Getting Paid!

Easy Home Staging Financial Strategies for Home Stagers

Barbara Jennings, CSS/CRS

ISBN 978-0-9618026-9-1

PRINTED IN THE UNITED STATES OF AMERICA
By AHAVA PRESS | AHAVA ENTERPRISES, INC.

Library of Congress No. TXu 1-588-005

Library of Congress Cataloging-in-Publication Data
Jennings, Barbara
   Getting Paid! Financial Strategies for Home Stagers/Barbara Jennings.

   1.   Home Staging Business.
   2.   Real Estate – Home Staging.
   3.   Interior Redesign Business.
   4.   Home Based Business.
   5.   Finances – Money.
   6.   Interior Decorating.

09 10 11 12 13 14 15 16 17 18 19 20 21 22 23 24 25

Table of Contents

1 - Getting Paid!
How to Make Sure You Get What You're Worth

Negotiation for what you want is a tricky process. Many people have many different styles of negotiating; some styles are effective and others are not. While the goal of all negotiations, in a perfect world, should be to end up with a result that is positive and beneficial for all parties concerned, this is not a perfect world.

All too often, each party strives to get as much benefit for themselves as they can, without regard to what the other parties might derive. Let's face facts. We're all pretty much self-serving when it comes to business and few people look out for the interests of anyone but themselves.

So this begs the question: How does one negotiate successfully, protecting one's own rights and interests, but yet reach a final agreement that is acceptable to all parties concerned. The answer is not easy; nor is it simple. Books have been written devoted to this topic.

I am going to reference some of the experiences I've had in my own business and unrelated income producing strategies as I think might pertain to this subject and be of some kind of value to you. Please bear in mind that to really learn how to negotiate effectively in business, you should consider getting some books on the subject written by negotiating experts. I do not claim to be an expert. But I have gained some insights and developed many procedures over the 38+ years I've been in business which I hope will be of value to you.

First of all, let me say that every time you negotiate with someone, whether verbally or on paper, it is a new experience and there are no rules. Whether you're buying a product or service from someone, or whether they are buying a product or service from you, there are no rules except for the ones you put in place for yourself. None. So you have to tread carefully, with planning and wisdom. You have to set your rules and stick to them.

Don't Act Like an Elephant

Have you ever noticed that elephants are restrained in place by a small stake in the ground and a thin rope or chain? Have you ever wondered why the elephant doesn't try to break such a weak resistance? The reason is that elephants have a very long memory. When they were babies they were restrained by small stakes and ropes or chains. They have never forgotten this as they grew to be adult elephants.

It has never dawned on the elephant that they have grown taller and more powerful and that they could easily break the restraints and leave at any time. They are controlled by their minds and the memories they have retained since their childhood.

You are not an elephant. You have the ability to reason and think and discard memories or thoughts and belief systems from the past that are no longer valid. As you read through the concepts of this manual, I want you to ask yourself if there is anything you are doing or failing to do that is based on a set of rules and regulations, obstacles and restraints that you formed a long time ago and never re-evaluated. I want you to recognize that you may very well be limiting your success and your ability to attain and retain profits because you are hanging on to old precepts that don't apply any longer.

What held you back in your youth has no bearing on your adult decisions and experience. So as you move through these ideas and concepts, continually challenge your old ideas, methods and processes to see if you are limiting yourself in any way. Test the old ways. Don't let your mind and your preconceived notions stop you from adapting, changing, improving and renewing everything about you and your business. You have the power to change anything you want to change.

Know What You're Worth – Set Your Rules

If you don't know what you're worth, how can you expect anyone else to know what you're worth? Knowing your true worth is your first priority. For many people this is a difficult concept. They have been devalued by other people for so long, they do not believe in their own value or worth. They have let, over time, other people dictate to them what they are worth. Chances are the people who are dictating to them are losers or highly critical people.

It's very easy to be critical of others. It's very easy to put other people down. Women are especially prone to do this, especially if they have a low self image. Their jealousy of other women gets the better of them and they find themselves being critical of others.

Let me give some examples of situations that have happened to me personally in the last 3 days which has prompted me to insert this section into this manuscript.

Periodically I go on line and type in my personal name and search on it just to see what pops up. You should probably do the same with your name. The more well known you become, the more links you will discover written by people you don't even know as well as people you know.

Hopefully all of it is good – but you may run across negative postings made by people that are false, mean spirited – even illegal. This was the case with me. As I was scrolling through pages, I found a link to a website where people can ask questions and get answers by those who are part of the forum. I was shocked to see that a young woman in New York had written a scathing paragraph, calling my training and programs a "scam" and using vulgarity in her comments.

Now this woman has never met me, never talked to me, never written me, never purchased a single product from me – yet she was writing terrible falsehoods and placing them on the internet to promote herself and her business.

Needless to say her company was contacted and threatened with a libel lawsuit. I received a verbal and written apology from her partner and the comments were quickly removed within 2 days. Eventually I received a written apology from her as well. In the end, your professional reputation is all you've got and unprofessional, unethical people can do you damage, even for a short period of time.

It's amazing to me how cruel and vicious people can be for self-promotional purposes – or simply because they CAN or because they refuse to accept responsibility for their own actions and want to blame others when things don't go as they expect or wish them to go. This happens more frequently than you would think.
So you've got to be ever vigilant and watch out for your reputation at all times. You don't need to become a fanatic about it, but you do need to be watchful.

You cannot do anything about how other people choose to conduct themselves and to try is wasted effort. But you CAN control your reactions and your own words and actions.

Hard as it is, sometimes you just have to remove people from having any impact on your life. If you find yourself in the company of negative, super critical people bent on your mental and emotional destruction, you need to severely limit their ability to have contact with you if at all possible.

Surrounding yourself with positive, uplifting people who will nurture you and encourage you and validate your self-worth is not only advantageous, it is essential to your success.

Cultivate the Habit of Being Complimentary

If you have not cultivated the HABIT of being complimentary, I strongly suggest you do so immediately. Anyone can become a positive, complimentary person.

Set a goal to compliment 5 people every day. Get in the habit of deliberately looking for people to bless with a warm hearted, genuine compliment. Do it in person. Do it over the phone. Do it in an email. Send an appreciative text message.

Post something positive, encouraging and helpful online. Send a beautiful, sentimental card.

The recipient could be your spouse. It could be a child, your mother, your father, a relative, a co-worker, a good friend, a person who has hurt you in the past. Everyone needs to be appreciated and there is so little of that any more. Avoid negativity at all cost as it not only hurts the other person –it really reflects badly on you.

No one wants to do business with a negative, critical, mean spirited person. Some people are so engrossed in their own feelings of superiority, so accustomed to being critical of  everything and every one, they might not even recognize that they have a serious problem.

If you're part of a competitive organization, be charitable to other people in the business. Believe me, it can come back to haunt you – and it just isn't nice anyway. If you witness evil comments and criticisms about others in forums, come to their defense in a professional manner. Don't attack other posters, but bring words of encouragement where ever you go and shed light that attracts people to you for your integrity, your willingness to help and share and your willingness to stand for what is right and fair.

Work on Your Self Image

A young friend of my son was adopted and while she says her Mom is a loving person and that she loves her very much, her Mom has been highly critical of her all her life. The extended family is also highly critical of her on every level. Because the assault comes from family members, whom she still needs in her life, she cannot remove herself totally from relationship with them, but she has dramatically cut back her visits, even preferring to hang out at my home on holidays. I feel genuinely bad for her.

Have respect and value for yourself and stop others from messing with your feelings about yourself. Self-respect has to begin in you and then spread to others.

You can control much of what goes on around you by setting your own rules of what you will or won't tolerate. That's where it begins. Set your boundaries and hold on to them and enforce them. It won't be long before you've eliminated much, if not all, of the criticism floating about you from the people you know and care about. As for strangers, you have little to no control over their behavior.

Once you know you are valuable, gifted, talented, knowledgeable, sincere, a blessing to others, then you're prepared to go to the next step.

Get Comfortable with Being Uncomfortable

Did you know that when you're growing as an individual, you are uncomfortable? Did you know that to become rich and successful you must first become uncomfortable? It's really true. The average person doesn't want to leave their comfort zone, so they are never willing to venture into unknown waters – unknown territories.

Living in your comfort zone will place you in a particular wealth zone. You cannot expand your wealth zone unless you expand your comfort zone. Risk taking is removing yourself from your comfort zone. If you don't take any risks, you will gain nothing more. Fear is what pushes you to refuse to take risks.

Making sure you get paid and taking the necessary steps to put into place the procedures and strategies that will help you ensure getting paid will undoubtedly take you outside your comfort zone – at least for a little while. But unless you get out of that comfort zone you will not move into a higher wealth zone.

Avoid Working For or With Critical People

If you meet someone and right off the bat you pick up on the fact that they are highly negative, highly critical or "lint picking", you're better off telling them that you are not a good fit for their project. Go on the offensive and tell them that your schedule will not allow you to take on their project.

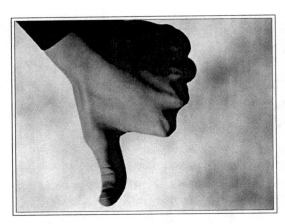 I can guarantee you that there are some people that will never ever be pleased, no matter what type of quality and service you give them. They will complain from the beginning. They will complain throughout the process. And they will complain after the project ends. Most certainly they will try to avoid payment.

It is their nature.

You will not be able to rise above their negativity, no matter how hard you try.

Have you ever known people who grew up with parents that could never be pleased? Perhaps your parents constantly complained about you and even when you did something outstanding, they still found a way to let you know your performance still fell short of their expectations.

You'd be amazed at how many people there are who are totally negative people and, of course, everything they touch turns out negative. I can pretty well guarantee you that if you associate with a complaining person you will live to regret it many times over.

There's just something about speaking out negativity into the life forces that acts like a boomerang and brings negativity back. On the rare occasions when I did not listen to my instincts and took on a project for a negative person, everything went wrong – and I do mean everything.

Vendors did not perform well. Deadlines were missed. Product was back-ordered or not available at all. People didn't show up for work. It was Murphy's Law every step of the way. Murphy's Law says that if something can go wrong, it will.

So do yourself an enormous favor and pass up projects (no matter how much you need the money) that you perceive to be involving negative clients.

Know What You Want to Get

Your second priority is to know in your mind or heart (and preferably on paper) exactly what you want to get out of any specific business transaction. You might know in advance what you're willing to pay or what you're willing to receive monetarily. You should establish a price range within which you're willing to go to work.

Once you know what you want and what you're willing to pay (or receive), then you need to establish a time limit. While a time limit can be any amount of time you agree to, it's common that agreements (or estimates or quotes) be good for 30 days, but this is not a hard and fast rule.

Then you need to decide whether any payment is due on the front end or not, or whether any payment is due throughout the process of acquiring or delivering the product or service.

In my present business, students and clients pay for products in advance using a credit card, check or money order. Most pay by credit card. The price is already established by me and it is non negotiable. When I render a service, however, the service is provided <u>in advance</u> of being paid (unless the amount due is substantial, in which case I require at least a 50% deposit).

In the home improvement business, when dealing with sub-contractors like roofing companies and the like, who are bound by state regulations, it is required by law that one pay no more than 10% deposit and the balance when the project is completed. But not all providers of goods and services are required by law to operate this way.

So in unregulated industries, like home staging and interior redesign, the rules and regulations are determined by the service provider and agreed to or re-negotiated by the client or customer. Again, I say, there are no rules.

Typically the marketplace will determine roughly what is a fair price and what terms are acceptable, but even then there are no set rules and both the providers and the clients must determine what is and is not acceptable to them. If there is a good deal of competition for the product or service, this tends to hold prices at a lower level than if there is little to no competition.

You've probably heard the term, "whatever the market will bear". Prices (just as we see in oil today and other commodities) are typically based on supply and demand. Whenever supply is greater than demand, prices are low. Whenever demand is greater than supply, then prices are high.

Since high priced oil is in the news so much as of this writing, one would think that when Americans drop their consumption by conserving their usage of gas and oil that the prices would drop. However, for every gallon we conserve, other growing economies around the globe are ready, willing and able to buy up what we don't use. So that's why the prices remain high and are likely to go higher.

When it comes to oil, there is always going to be far more demand for the product than there is a supply to meet that demand, so prices will only go higher in the future.

It's too bad the demand for home staging and redesign doesn't exceed the supply. We'd all be making a fortune without having to try. But this is not the case. In many cases, we've not only got to convince a prospect that our services and products are of value to them, we've got to educate them on what the service or product does.

This is not true of gasoline. We all know it moves cars and machinery. We all know that oil is used to create a multitude of products. And if you're not aware of it yet, oil is not only being used up on the planet, it's also harder to find and more expensive to get out of the ground.

So even if demand was not greater than supply, just the increased costs of getting oil would send the prices higher. Add to that the lower value of the dollar (and oil is valued in dollars), and you can see why we have record high.

But that's enough about oil and gasoline. I do want you to understand that everything in your business is open for negotiation – just about everything. So how well you negotiate depends on how prepared you are for the task and what you're willing to accept and what you're not willing to accept.

It's Not What the Market Will Bear

Some people teach you to call up the competition and in some kind of fake voice ask them, "How much do you charge?" This is not only silly, it's unprofessional. Then they will teach you to adjust your prices to whatever your competition is charging or lower than what the competition is charging to "beat the price". Also very silly.

The novice method of determining prices for goods and services is to charge whatever you think the market will bear. The idea promoted is that your prospect, your customer or competition will determine your price for you. Whatever they are willing to pay you is what you will charge. Well, this sounds reasonable but is it really reasonable?

I guess it's the easy way out of putting forth genuine effort to determine what you should charge. Perhaps you're one of those people who called up several other businesses with your survey. You got a range of pricing and you set yours somewhere in that range. You feel good about your price because you feel you're charging "what the market will bear". But that price could fall way below your break-even point and you could be losing money right and left.

You see, you can't ask the competition what their operating costs are. You have no idea what their break even point is, which could be quite different from yours. There are a zillion components that could affect their pricing upwards and downwards that you will never have a clue about.

And for the home staging and redesign industry there's an important factor to consider. The "what the market will bear" rule applies to commodities only. Commodities are products that don't differ much from vendor to vendor.

A Kodak Easy Share camera, for instance, is a commodity. This camera has an MSRP (manufacturer's suggested retail price). It will follow the Economics 101 rule of "what the market will bear" pretty nicely. It will be governed by the law of 'supply and demand'. Yes there will be fluctuations and sale prices, but by and large there will be a rather limited price range for this product. Economics 101 works well when you are talking about commodities. But it doesn't amount to very smart business for a consultant.

Here's the **real** rule, the consultant's rule - the rule you won't learn in Economics 101: The market doesn't set the selling price for you. YOU set the price. Ask yourself these questions:

- Why does Coca Cola sell for three times the price of generic colas?
- How come Rolex sells watches for $50,000 when you can get a very nice watch for $100?
- Why did some people pay $15,000 to cross the Atlantic on the Concord when a jet plane could have got them there for about $500?

You're going to have to learn how to effectively market your services. You're going to have to learn how to differentiate your products and services and create the aura that they are MORE than a commodity. You have to learn how to identify features that benefit your clients. It is those benefits that add value to your product or service.

Coke is the *real* thing. The Rolex brand is a symbol of power and wealth. The Concord was for speed lovers. Anything perceived to be of a higher value commands a higher price.

The wallet or the credit card will only be exchanged for something that has a higher perceived value. So if your product or service is worth exactly what you are charging for it, no one will hire you or purchase your product. So then what usually happens is that you will drop your price until the value of your product exceeds the price, and then you'll sell it. What I want to teach you is to increase the value of your product or service until the price seems insignificant. Then you will start to enjoy a profitable business.

Do you see what I'm getting at? You can base your pricing on your competition, charging blindly for your services and hope you're not getting ripped off in the process. You can hope your competition isn't offering a special deal that you know nothing about. You can walk in fear and base everything on what you think your competition is doing – or you can make sure you're doing something that is not only quite different and better and therefore worth a whole lot more. You can put yourself into a niche of one.

That's what I have done. You will not see another trainer in the industry that offers anything remotely close to my programs and products. I am in a niche of one. It is I who determined the value and worth of every product I sell and I don't let the competition dictate my value nor my pricing. That would be fool hardy.

And remember one other thing. Your competition probably knows less about this subject than you do. Your competitors probably have no clue as to their break even point and their true costs of doing business. So don't assume that your competition knows more than you know. Your competition probably set their prices based on making the same silly phone calls you made. And they've based their pricing on companies that have since gone out of business. How smart is that?

In our industry, there's a lot of confusion out there when it comes to setting price points, especially in the home staging arena. They look at what every other stager is charging and they hope and pray that they can make money at those prices. I say they are inviting failure at every turn.

Here's the right way to price your products and services.

Decide how much money YOU want to make. Offer a terrific service along with any products you sell. Figure out ALL your costs of doing business, even down to the rubber bands you purchase and the staples you use. Come up with a selling price that makes your dreams come true. Ask yourself if you would pay that amount to get someone with your talent to solve your problems. This is how you adopt a real marketer's mindset. Create so much value for your product that your clients beg to hire you. Don't take every project that comes your way. Some will be a waste of your time and energy and some will rob you of your peace. By being discriminating, you're also creating value and a mind-set of exclusivity for your service. People love to pay extra for exclusivity.

Assumptions Are Not Your Friends

Business transactions can turn sour based on someone's assumptions or expectations. Assumptions and expectations are not your friends, no matter which side of the fence you're on.

How often have you made an assumption about a person you just met only to find out a little later that your assumption had no merit or factual basis? It happens all the time. That's because people sometimes present themselves one way at first when in reality they are really quite different.

 But it also happens because we place unrealistic expectations upon them based on our own desires and needs. This is unfair. We cannot assume that other people will rise up to our expectations of them. We don't like it when we're unfairly judged, but we're all prone to be unfair to other people. We don't mean to be, usually, but it is part of our nature.

We all look at life and circumstances and other people through rose colored glasses, and we evaluate them and situations based on our life experiences to date, whether good experiences, neutral experiences or bad experiences.

Some people are too trusting. Some people are too suspicious. Some people are in between the two extremes. And just as we are trusting or suspicious of other people, they feel the same way about us. So there's the dilemma.

If you stop to think about it, when you've been suspicious of someone else, your feelings quite often prove to be unfounded. But they can just as easily be found to be true. That's because, at heart, we are all self-focused individuals, looking out primarily for our selves or our loved ones. We think of ourselves as fair minded, honest people. But when push comes to shove, and certainly when money is involved, we tend to be greedy and self-serving.

So we need to be careful.

We would all get along so much better and be able to transact so much more business if everyone tried harder to be fair to themselves, but also fair to the other person.

So my advice to you is to attempt, whenever possible, to negotiate your business transactions in a win/win manner. Know what you want and need to get from a transaction, but try hard to see the other person's viewpoint and circumstance. Try to put yourself in their shoes and look at the situation as they look at it.

This will help you steer clear of negotiations that are one-sided. It's not wise to be in a transaction that favors only you any more than to be in a transaction which favors only the other side. The best transactions are when all parties are happy and all parties will never be happy until or unless they have been promised (in writing) to receive something of value that they feel is fairly priced.

Never enter a transaction when you feel you are being taken advantage of. Because if you start out feeling at a disadvantage, your negative feelings will only increase as time goes by. Never enter a transaction if you surmise the other party feels at a disadvantage, because as sure as snow melts, their feelings will melt into gushers of negativity and there will be constant complaints. You'll likely end up with someone who cannot be pleased under any circumstances.

When I sell a product over the internet, I have no way of knowing whether the client feels the deal is fair or not. I've tried to present a detailed explanation about every product or service I provide, but I have no control over whether a visitor to my website actually reads and understands what has been written. But I have to assume that they would not purchase at all if they felt uncomfortable with any part of the transaction. This is much different from negotiating a business transaction in person with an agreement or contract. So I'm obviously not talking about internet transactions or point of purchase sales made where the customer can see and touch the product before buying.

I'm merely talking about the negotiations between two or more parties dealing with each other face to face for the exchange of goods and/or services that are to be provided based on the independent negotiating of all parties involved.

I always try to give my prospects and clients an "A" grade to start. Whether they keep the grade or not will be determined by their actions and words from that point forward. Naturally when you give an "A", you hope they will live up to your expectations of what an A grade implies. Naturally your expectations are yours alone. And you can decide what those expectations are. You can also change those expectations whenever you choose.

But never forget, your prospect or client is also giving you a grade as well. But you're going to assume the grade is also an "A" -- but it might not be an "A". It might be a "B". One would think that no one would hire you if they did not believe you were an "A+" candidate, but then again their expectations of you are always going to be quite different from your expectations of yourself. And everyone has their own standards of what individual grades represent.

So the more you can hammer out the expectations on both sides of the transaction, and define them clearly, so that everyone is "on the same page", so to speak, the better off the transaction will play out. The more expectations are left to chance or not clearly defined, the greater the chances that problems will arise and someone is going to get unhappy. When all expectations are defined, they should be memorialized in writing, so that no one can claim them to be other than agreed to.

Written agreements always take precedence over verbal agreements, so if you find you've put in place a written agreement, and then for any reason whatsoever that written agreement is mutually changed, the changes must also be in writing as an Addendum and the Addendum must be attached to the original agreement for all parties. If the changes are not put in writing once a written contract exists, they will not hold up in court. A judge will only consider what is in writing. So unless all parties were to acknowledge that changes had been agreed to, they will not be considered part of the agreement unless they are in writing.

Any ambiguity in a written agreement goes against the person who drew up the agreement, so if you put an agreement in writing, it's best to be as clear as possible in the wording as to what each party must contribute (and receive in return), because if a judge believes there was no "meeting of the minds", the judge will rule against the party that drew up the written agreement. If an agreement is verbal, a judge will lean in favor of the party whose story is most believable and in keeping with the law.

This is why I advise everyone, particularly in the home staging business, to seek the help of a good local attorney, who knows the laws of your state or county, so that your rights can be adequately understood and protected in your written contracts. But also so that there will be no wiggle room open for interpretation by the other party or by a judge.

2 – Getting Paid!
How to Make Sure You're Taking the Right Steps

It's More Than Getting an Agreement

I've read my share of books teaching how to sell more effectively, but I've only seen one that, after listing the major components of selling, covers the most important subject of all – how you make sure you get paid.

Typically they will tell you this:

1) Have a product or service to sell
2) Locate your target market
3) Implement your marketing method
4) Meet with the prospect and close the sale

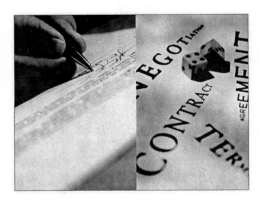

And by "close the sale", they mean to get the client to sign on the dotted line. But as you may already know, there is a difference between getting a client to sign a contract and actually getting them to write you a check for services. And the greater amount of time that passes between the signing of a contract and when the money is due, the greater the chances grow that you might not see that check. The higher the amount you are to be paid, the higher the chances are that you will *not* be paid — at least not in the amount and by the date you should be paid.

So the most neglected subject remains:

5) How to get paid.

Generally speaking, getting paid for services from a redesign client is easy. You're right there in their home and just that fact alone will cause most home owners to pull out their checkbook or wallet when you're done. No matter how they feel at the moment, whether they think you're worth what you charge or not, they're not going to want to take a chance on you refusing to leave and any ensuing confrontation over payment (or the lack thereof).

However, getting paid for a staging project can be a whole different can of worms or set of challenges. Home staging can involve many days and hours or your time. It can involve the costs of renting furnishings, hiring sub contractors and vendors, and it can involve a host of other costs, both large and small.

So your exposure on the subject of getting paid is much greater. Your risks are definitely higher; but of course so are your profits. That's why it is crucial to approach any real estate agent or homeowner from a position of power, with a bit of intimidation right from the moment you meet. This is another reason why you don't want to be judged by your portfolio alone, without being evaluated in person at the very same time.

You see, if you want to increase the chances of getting paid, you've got to be viewed by all other parties as a true professional — and not just any professional. You've got to be viewed from a position of power. Because if the other people in the deal do not perceive you as a person of power, they will disrespect you and likely try to intimidate you.

 The moment you feel intimated in any way, you will appear weak. Your words can be strong, but your entire body language, subtext and aura that you project will scream out, "I'm weak. I'm open to being taken advantage of. Don't respect me because I don't have much respect for myself."

Most people have no idea what the power of intimidation can do – both to help you and to hinder you. It's all about image – which is all about power (or perceived power). It boils down to how you *position* yourself. And in a minute I'm going to teach you *3 types of Positioning* that you can decide to implement.

You see, it doesn't matter if you have a ton of knowledge or talent. None of these issues (knowledge/talent) means much if your positioning (image) is weak. I've said in other writings how important it is that people like you. But it's just as important that they respect you. Weak people will never get respect in the business world. Young people will find it more difficult to command respect.

Never lose sight of the fact that people are basically greedy and materialistic. And while they may say they believe in a win/win business arrangement, they all too often will try to wiggle out of financial arrangements if there is a delay in timing from the signing of the contract to the completion of the work. I know far too many consultants (even including myself on occasion) who have invested many hours into a project for a client, only to have the deal unwind and watch as the client tries to back out without paying a cent. I have occasionally had to file a small claims lawsuit.

You don't want this to happen to you. So I'm going to teach you some methods to help prevent that from happening. But bear in mind that there is no iron clad method to prevent a client from trying to keep from paying you. But there are important steps you can take to offset the chance of having to meet them in court.

And it begins, first and foremost, with your image. They must see you and believe you to be operating from a position of power. There are two kinds of power. There is *real power* and there is *perceived power*.

Some people are wealthy; their wealth gives them an automatic degree of "real power" because it affords them the ability to have "staying power". Staying power is the ability to ride things out no matter how long they take to resolve. You might not have wealth, so you've got to create "perceived power" instead until you become wealthy - well, not instead of, as you've got to continue to exude perceived power even after you become wealthy.

So here are the essential three elements of perceived power that I promised to teach you. You might even think of a few more elements to add as you grow in your business, but these are the absolute basics.

Legal Positioning

The first type of power you can put into place in your business is *legal positioning*. Any time you need to you can always hire an attorney to attend a meeting to represent your interests, but this can be costly and unnecessary on projects of a smaller profit margin. But bear in mind that just having an attorney present creates a huge amount of *legal positioning* on your side.

There is something about getting attorneys together that changes the dynamic of any meeting. Attorneys will battle it out when they are in their "battle stance" and there is automatic respect that flows back and forth between them. They can then leave the scene of the battle, almost arm and arm and go have a drink together. Strange. But this is how they are.

But since most of the time you're probably not going to want to pay an attorney to represent you, you've got to create that same kind of respect yourself.

The first legal tool you'll need to have is a contract (agreement) that will seal your fee in writing. Never ever let an agent or a homeowner talk you into going ahead and working without a signed agreement. If you work on a "handshake" basis or a "verbal" basis, you're just asking them to cut you out of the deal down the road. This is the first sign of operating from a weak posture. So don't fall into the trap of having a signed document for one client and not for all your clients. Make it a *company policy* to make every client sign an agreement that stipulates what you will be paid, when you will be paid, and what is expected of you, and what is expected of your client in return. And make them sign it. No exceptions.

You might write this short poem on a piece of paper and carry with you at all times to remind you of this important operating philosophy:

**With a written agreement
You have a prayer;
With a verbal agreement
You have nothing but air.**

If a client refuses to sign such a document, head for the door and don't look back. Because if you don't, I promise you that you will probably live to regret it.

The second legal tool is to use *certified mail*. Whenever you use certified mail to submit a document to your client, they sit up and take notice and mentally and emotionally recognize your role in the deal at a deeper level. They are not stupid. They surely recognize that should a lawsuit arise because of failure to pay you the agreed to amount, that you will have certified slips and letters to bring to court to back up any claims you make. The last attorney I hired sent me a letter after every court appearance documenting the fact that he had appeared on the client's behalf. He can get away with send such a notice by regular mail. I suggest you use certified mail.

Again, make a decision to use certified mail in all of your dealings, not just some. Never rely on email or the US postal service and a postage stamp. You always want to have a way to prove that the client got the document. So even if you are in the client's presence, and they sign the documents in your presence, it is prudent to make copies of the documents and send them to the client by certified mail (as a back up).

This is important – not just because you want to have plenty of evidence should you go to court – you want to *avoid* lawsuits – and this is the best way to avoid them altogether.

Lastly, this business does not require you to have a real estate license. But it should go without saying that if you have such a license, this adds further to your legal positioning and you should definitely let your prospects and clients know that you have a real estate license if you have one. I would not go get one, however, unless I wanted to sell homes. As long as you restrict your business dealings to the art of home staging and interior redesign, you do not need a license of any kind (other than a business license and possibly a resale license).

Abstract Positioning

One of the key ingredients in establishing *abstract positioning* is not how you look and sound, though these areas are extremely important as well. But aside from creating a powerful, quality portfolio, it's your calling card and the strength of it and the impact it has on the recipient.

Most times someone who goes into business gets a business card. I've shown you examples of typical business cards in my book, *Staging Portfolio Secrets*. I even showed you an example of my cat's business card.

But what if you didn't do what was standard and expected? What if your business card was actually a brochure – and not the 3-fold brochures like I showed you in my book *Staging Portfolio Secrets*? What if your calling card was the most expensive, beautifully conceived and developed brochure anyone had ever seen?

What if the brochure cost you $5 each or more to produce because it was that exquisite? What kind of positioning or image do you think that would create for you? And what if you were really choosey about whom you gave the brochure to? Remember, you never want to come across as desperate or hungry to land a project. You want the prospect to feel lucky if you accept THEM as a client, not the other way around.

If you were to design yourself a brochure that grabbed the prospect in such a way that they wanted to display it on their desk or in their home in some manner, wouldn't that say an awfully lot about you?

Do you think anyone would question you and your talent after getting a brochure like that? And if you hardly mentioned who you were in it, do you think that would come across as classy and a cut above? That alone will make you stand out above all others in the business.

And what if your "calling card brochure" was hard bound, like a book (or at the very least, a booklet with a glossy color cover)? Would that impress anyone?

Picture a book (hard bound) the size of 10" x 10", with a totally black cover except for a breathtaking full-color photo of a gorgeous home or even a breathtaking view of Earth from the Apollo spacecraft. It opens from the bottom up, not from right to left.

Your name is not on the front. Your name is not on the inside front, nor is it on the first page.

The first 4 pages say (each line is on a page by itself):

Home
         To the Individual ..... *A Place of Ownership*
         To the Family .... *A Place of Belonging*

         To the Wise .... *A Place of Investment*

The fifth page shows a telescopic view of your city or town or some landmark recognizable to all who live there.

It is not until the next page that your name appears.

Do you think anything much needs to be said by that point? Without saying a word, your brochure/book has presented you as a real *somebody*. Anyone who would go to such an expensive effort to create such a brochure must be *someone successful who knows what they're doing and should be given attention.*

Throughout the book you could include brief statements alluding to your general expertise. You could include a few dramatic photos, your logo and a handful of testimonials (just a few powerful ones).

This type of calling card is intimidating. It isn't meant to be sent to everyone, however. You should be discriminating, especially in the beginning.

It isn't meant for the recipient to fully understand who you are or what you do. It's merely to make a strong, unforgettable statement that you are *someone* worthy of tremendous respect.

Before you ever agree to meet with a prospect, you have made sure that they have received your brochure. You're never in a hurry. You're never anxious. You never chase them – you make them feel they need to chase you. Later, if you agree to meet with them at all, your presence and your professional portfolio work to seal the deal, if you choose to add them as a client.

After you know they have received the brochure and it's had its chance to impact them in a powerful way, you call and ask questions. You never ever agree to meet with them until and unless you have gotten enough questions answered by the prospect to judge whether the property is worthy of your time and talent. And you will follow up your questions with this statement, "I would have to personally inspect the property before making any commitment."

In other words, you make them prove to you that their property is worthy of being added to your list of projects and that they very well could be turned down by you. You see you're not just interested in whether your prospect wants to hire a home stager, or needs to do so; you want to know whether there's going to be enough need for your services to bring you a handsome fee and where you can actually make a difference, otherwise it's not in your best interest to proceed further.

If you feel the house is not salable, or if you feel the client isn't the type of person you want to be associated with, or if you feel there isn't going to be enough profit in the project to warrant your attention and expertise, then you'll turn the prospect down and walk away and move on to the next, better situation.

That by itself makes you *someone* to be respected.

You'll be doing yourself and your prospect a huge favor to make sure on the front end that you're a "good fit" for each other. If you're not a good fit for each other, neither one of you will be happy, guaranteed. By being choosey about the projects you accept, you will also raise the level of respect they have for you – and this is essential in the process of making sure you'll get paid.

Eventually you'll even be able to say on the telephone, or in your brochure, that you only accept 3 out of every 10 projects

HOME . . .

(numbers will vary), which further suggests that the prospect (and their property) must prove to you that THEY are worthy of your expertise, not the other way around.

When you get to this level, you're operating in true *abstract positioning*.

Here's a variation on that theme. See how dramatic you can make a short book or brochure or other type of presentation by using a strong background color, such as black and keeping your imagery and text short and to the point.

HOME TOWN . . .
A PLACE FOR FAMILIES

Pictured here is a landmark of my home town, Huntington Beach, featuring the downtown pier, as my town is famous for surfing and surfing events. You would instead include a photo of where you live that would be easily recognized as representing your city, town or state.

Then you make it more personal by bringing it down to the individual and family and individual goals. You'll want to have a variety of pictures of different rooms in a typical home.

TO THE INDIVIDUAL . . .
A PLACE OF OWNERSHIP

You might also want to vary the styles that you show as you will not know the personal tastes of any one reading your materials and hopefully you can hit a responsive chord with at least one picture you show.

TO THE FAMILY . . .
A PLACE OF BELONGING

Try to select pictures that draw the viewer into the picture if you can. Of course you can only work with the pictures you have. But choose pictures that have unique angles, that hopefully show a nice view out a window or that create a mood or feeling. If you have no pictures whatsoever, you can purchase stock photographs or check with friends, family and others to see if you can use their photos (assuming they are excellent photos).

Make sure the rooms pictured are not cluttered.

TO THE WISE . .
A PLACE OF INVESTMENT

You can even use a stack of postcards (regular or oversized). You can print anything at any size and in any shape. Of course, the more you veer from the norm (size and shape), the more you will add to your cost of printing, however, odd shapes and sizes will add to the appeal, drama and intrigue, which adds to your making a bolder statement than your competitors. But you still want to compare costs with the ultimate value before splurging to the max.

If you can have two pictures of a living room or family room, one picture of a bedroom and one picture of a kitchen, you will have succeeded in giving a nice balanced overview of the rooms most often staged.

Then include your logo (I'm including my certification emblems here as blatant advertising examples) and business name (I'm choosing my website but you can use your website

DECORATE-REDECORATE.COM

or your business name or your personal name) **after** the prospect gets well into the piece of literature you've put together. By this time they should be thoroughly impressed with your message and ripe to see your logo and business name.

Following such a strong introduction, you would list the benefits of doing business with you and some impressive testimonials, statistics and all of your contact information. Get the idea?

Performance Positioning

Once you have your legal positioning and your abstract positioning in place, you want to back them up with your *performance positioning*. You get this by deciding in advance to provide the absolute best products and services in the industry. You commit yourself to treating every client as if they were your *only* client and give them the absolute best service you can possibly render.

This is a commitment you will make. And if you're not prepared to make such a commitment, you should quit the business because no one wants someone messing around with the industry's reputation, deliberately choosing to give inferior service.

You need to make a commitment to becoming impressive – so that you will truly deserve any compensation that comes your way. So should you ever land in court, you not only have your legal positioning in place, but you will have it backed up with superior performance as well. Just do your job well. That's all.

This means that you'll need to be very organized and detailed. You want to become so good at what you do that you make it virtually impossible for anyone to say, without suffering tremendous guilt feelings, that you had not done enough to earn your fee.

This means you become unwavering in your determination to always do the right thing. Sometimes the right thing may cost you some money, but it should never ever cost you your reputation. When faced with a dilemma, I suppose it is human nature to resort to handling it in an instinctual fashion. This happens out of panic or being unsure as to what to do.

But I can tell you from personal experience that you never have to regret handling something in the *right* way. As Dustin Hoffman's character said in *Scent of a Woman,* he always knew, without exception, what the right way was. But he never took it; he always took the easy way. And for many people, the easy way (or so they think) is to run away and avoid the problem altogether.

But you will not do this. You will commit yourself to always doing what is right, even if it is a bit painful. This too will increase your chances of *avoiding* court.

Recognizing the Saleable Property

Before accepting a project you need to inspect it to make sure it is in reasonable condition so that it can be presentable in the near future to be sold. Not all properties are saleable. The older the home, the harder it is to sell. Most properties are sold within the first 10-12 years of being built and thereafter the task becomes more difficult until, or unless, the property eventually becomes a historical site.

If you're like me, and I think most people are like me, you'd rather purchase a house that is in mint condition, or as close to that as you can get (unless you're in the business of flipping properties). So the older a home is, the more repair work and upgrades it likely needs to be salable.

You might not want to tackle such a property or might not be able to pull it off, even if you wanted to do so. For this reason, and many others, you need to insist on seeing and inspecting the property before granting the owner permission to avail themselves of your services.

Notice I say "avail themselves of your services" and not the other way around. If you have positioned yourself properly, you have created the aura that the prospective client must somehow EARN your willingness to do business. When you've accomplished this desire in your prospect, you are in the best position to command respect and manage the project the way you see fit rather than the other way around.

Depending on how you structure your business and how invested in a project you are willing to become, you may find that you'll decide to pass up many of the projects you have opportunity to inspect.

 A client of mine needed to sell an older home due to a divorce. I went over to give my expertise on staging the home and she was going to do all of the work. I reworked the furniture and accessories throughout the home, gave advice on things to fix and replace and what to purchase to complete the staging. She followed my advice as best she could though she was on a meager budget.

But although the inside of the house looked great, my friend couldn't get anyone to even enter the house due to the age of the home, other newer construction in the area and the sheer amount of upgrading and repair that still needed to be done, with a good deal of that demanded by the front yard and crumbling roof.

Six months later the home was in foreclosure, even after two significant price reductions and all our staging efforts. There just are going to be some properties that aren't going to sell. You've got to face reality and so does the homeowner; many people refuse to accept reality. So you need to be selective in the projects you will accept. I already knew it was not good use of my time – but one will make concessions for friends.

You don't want to build a portfolio based on un-saleable homes. This will rob you of your enthusiasm, energy and confidence and it will not give you great stories to tell to help you land more projects.

Owners who are desperate will try their hardest to hook you into a deal based on fantasy and often try to get you to agree to bind your fee to a successful sale or upon "closing". If the property never sells, you never get paid for your services. If the owner changes their mind and pulls the property from the market, you also don't get paid. So beware these types of tactics. Use the services of a good attorney in such cases.

A homeowner is never going to admit that their property is beyond hope of a sale. One clue to their personal belief about the house is whether they focus their conversation on telling you how much it cost them to upgrade, build or decorate it already. What an owner has invested to date in a property means nothing to a prospective buyer. The owner could easily have spent too much on the house or spent money in unproductive ways.

While there are many reasons why a homeowner becomes desperate to sell, this can also be a clue as to whether the property is saleable or not. Being desperate is good for you because it brings into focus more sharply their need for your services. But being overly desperate is not good for you because the budget to accomplish what's needed isn't likely to be there and there are more temptations for the owners to take advantage of you and find ways not to pay you in the end.

This is why you will always be in a more power position when you say, "I will have to personally inspect the property before making any commitment." Once you have decided to take on the project you say, "I believe I can *do something* with this property." Never promise that the property will definitely sell and most specifically never promise that the property will sell for a higher amount. While it's typical that staged homes sell faster and often for higher amounts, you cannot and should not guarantee that to anyone. So what you say and how you say it becomes very important. It's all in the phrasing.

Your competition will more than likely venture out on a limb that may very well get cut down by over-promising what can be done. This is dangerous because you don't want to wind up with the client suing you and claiming that you misled them. By saying, "I can *do something*" you retain a bit of mystery surrounding you and your talents and don't let yourself open for problems in the future.

I also advise you to have a detailed form with you when you arrive that you can use to fill in as you inspect the property to help you discern whether it is a good project for you to accept or not. Since I've already included a host of forms for this purpose in another manual I won't be including them here. But you can easily draw up your own to aid you in dissecting the worthiness of a property for your services.

How Distance Helps You

I hate to do projects that are some distance from my office. I just hate to commute. But in reality clients tend to value the opinion of someone not in the area more than those in their local community. Silly? Yes. But it's a proven fact.

Strange as it may seem, the greater the distance is between your office and your project (client's house), the more of an "expert" you become in the mind of the client. It doesn't matter if the client is a real estate agent or the homeowner. For some reason people think that someone coming from afar knows more than someone coming from nearby. And the farther you travel, the more your prospect or client feels obligated to do business with you.

But you still have to factor the travel time into your quotes and should your own sub-contractors and vendors have a significant distance to travel as well, their charges for services is bound to increase. Still in all, the greater respect a client has for you and the more you make sure you have positioned yourself in a powerful way in their mind, the less risk you will have when it comes to making sure you are paid (and paid promptly) for your services.

Focusing on Benefits Rather Than Features

When it comes to marketing your services, next to the pictures you show, the MOST important elements are the WORDS you use to sell your services or your products.

People don't visit a website or look at your portfolio just for pretty pictures or funky design elements -- they come looking for INFORMATION. They don't set appointments with you based on pictures. They want facts and figures and even more than that, they want to know how you will benefit them.

That's why you need to make sure to give them the information they need, in words that catch their attention and compel them to want your services. Look for ways to tap their emotional side as well as their intellectual side.

Unfortunately, when it comes time to writing copy for your portfolio, letters, brochures and so forth, many consultants commit a FATAL mistake: they focus on the features of their product or service -- in other words, what it does, how it operates, or what it looks like.

STAGERS CREATE AMBIENCE

However, good sales copy doesn't solely focus on the features of the product or service -- it focuses on the *user*, and how he or she will benefit from using the product or service.

The difference between a feature and a benefit is this: A feature is something the product has or does, while a benefit is something it does for you.

- A **FEATURE** is one of the components or functions of your product or service.

- A **BENEFIT** is a way in which your product or service improves the life of the prospect or client.

In other words, a benefit is an answer to the question, "What's in it for *me*?"
If that distinction is hard for you to grasp, just keep in mind that benefits are directly related to features. You can usually list all your features first and then go through your list and identify the corresponding benefits. Here are some examples of features and their corresponding benefits:

- **Feature:** Using the furnishings you already have in the home.
- **Benefit:** You save money; and don't have to make any difficult decisions.

- **Feature:** Half day or full day services.
- **Benefit:** You save countless hours so you have more time with your family or more time to relax.

- **Feature:** Objective consultation services
- **Benefit:** We help the maximum number of buyers fall in love with your home on sight leading to a potential bidding war.

- **Feature:** Inexpensive, insured rental furniture upon request.
- **Benefit:** Take your furniture with you and eliminate the risk of damage or theft of your most prized possessions and valuables.

If you're still having trouble distinguishing between the two, ask yourself this: Did you buy a car with air conditioning just because it had air conditioning -- or because it would keep you cool and comfortable on hot days? Did you buy a minivan simply because it had anti-lock brakes and airbags -- or because it was safer for you and your family? Will you sell your SUV now because of its lack of features or because you want to save money on gasoline?

Does this make sense?

Benefits are not "quality and service" or "cheapest." They are the answer to "What's in it for *me*?" or "Why should I keep reading?" or "How will hiring you make *my* life better?"

People don't want food -- they want to stay alive. So food companies have made their fortunes by stressing how their food solves the problem of staying alive and tasting really good all at the same time. People don't want to store gold –

but they want to hedge against a devalued dollar, so they invest in gold during troubled times.

By offering benefits instead of features, you will create a higher perceived value, which will translate into more projects and sales for your business. And that's a huge benefit for you and why you got into the business in the first place, right?

Important Points to Make to Real Estate Agents

The features and benefits you would pitch to a real estate agent will be different from those you communicate to the homeowner. Everyone wants the house to sell quickly and for maximum profit. That goes without saying. A higher selling price means more profit for the owner; it also means a higher commission for the agent.

But think of valuable points you can mention to the real estate agent or broker that could put them completely on your side and either hiring you or at least recommending you to the homeowner.

- I'll make sure the properties you represent are always in turnkey condition prior to an open house or putting into the multiple listings or online websites.
- Since you can only make a first impression once, why not make it the best among all available properties.
- Since you can only make one lasting impression once, let me make sure it is one that motivates an offer.
- Increase client confidence by presenting yourself as an agent who has the staff and sub-contractors at your disposal to manage any detail small or large.
- Let me be the person with the bad news. Preserve your client/agent relationship and allow me alert the seller to needed repairs or adjustments.

- Let me help you increase your listings. You can effectively advertise your usage of my services.
- Your respect among other agents will rise as their confidence in your quality listings increases.
- Allow me to reduce your advertising budget by increasing the chances to move your properties quickly and for higher selling prices.
- Time is money. Let me save you incredible amounts of time and frustration.
- Specialization is essential in today's competitive world. Rely on my expertise in design and free yourself for concentration in your area of expertise.

Separating the Serious from the Non-Serious

Go to every appointment knowing in advance that it very well may not lead to a project for you. Many people just want to pick your brain. They hope you'll divulge valuable information which they won't have to pay to get.

I remember well the day my partner and I drove about 45 minutes to an appointment with a gentleman who wanted to discuss the feasibility of doing business together, promising that while he couldn't divulge certain specifics over the phone, he would do so in person. Hogwash.

Naively we went and allowed this person and his assistant to literally pick our brains. We answered all their questions but when it was our turn to get our questions answered, all we got was "that's proprietary and we can't divulge it unless we pick your company to do business with". Well, you know how that turned out, right?

To this day I mentally kick myself for being so foolish. Not only did we give up a great deal of proprietary information we usually closely guard, but we literally wasted a half day of our valuable time and energy that we'll never get back.

Here's a clue about how to spot the serious from the non-serious. They all tend to act, talk and behave in the exact same manner. All you have to do is ask them over the phone (before you ever set an appointment with them) as to the guidelines or budget they plan to operate by. If they say, "We have no guidelines" or "We have no budget" and that "We are open to suggestions and willing to consider anything", then you know that you probably are not talking to a serious prospect.

Most serious prospects have a definite guideline or budget and they know exactly what they're looking for. Serious prospects don't want to waste time and get down to business right away.

The non-serious prospects operate by the philosophy that they have "everything to gain and nothing to lose" by talking to a host of people. They want to know what deals are "out there" or what insider information they can pick up on for free.

This is another reason why you want to pre-develop a host of questions – even the "hard questions" – and ask them over the phone before you ever set an appointment. You need to weed out the non-serious prospect as quickly as possible without offending them. By asking questions, you'll be able to privately determine whether it is worth it to you to agree to an appointment or not.

If the answer is "no", you simply tell them that you are not a "good fit" for them. Perhaps you can refer them to someone else instead. But the idea is to preserve your time for truly serious prospects – the kind of people you want to associate with – the kind of people who will appreciate your time and talent and pay you appropriately for what you bring to the table.

Curiosity seekers and free information seekers infiltrate every industry and ours is no exception. To get ahead, you've got to weed them out and avoid being misled by whatever promises they initially make to you. If I had a dime for every person who promised me *more* business on the backend if I would just discount to them on the front end, I'd seriously be richer than I am today. Don't fall for future promises. Most of the time they are worthless and the promises are really a disguise for some other ulterior purpose.

I make it a point in my consultations to never give a discount ever. I have carefully arrived at what I feel is a fair price already. To discount my price is to devalue my time, my expertise and my value. I won't do it. I've also found that when someone asks for a discount and I refuse one, they usually go ahead and do business with me anyway. More about this in an upcoming section titled "Can You Pass the Flinch Test?"

You should also know that no matter how wise you think you have become, and no matter how carefully you try to protect your position in business, there is always someone out there who has figured out a clever angle to get past you or get one over on you. So don't be naïve to think that you'll always be able to sort out the good prospect from the bad. You won't be successful 100% of the time. But if you follow these tips and guidelines, you'll at least minimize your risks and maximize your gains. And that's the secret to being successful in the stock market – it's also the secret to being successful in business as a home stager.

Arriving at an Agreement

I've written over and over again in my manuals the importance of getting agreements in writing and getting them signed and dated. Many stagers draw up complicated legal documents (contracts) and even refer to them as contracts. Well, you'll have to make the decision as to whether you want to work with a long contract full of legalese or not.

There is value in having one should you wind up in court. However, most people are leery of contracts and you may scare off your prospect if you whip out some long, detailed document in small type. Instead, you could opt for a one page "understanding" which you have them sign. Whether you call your documents a "contract" or an "understanding" doesn't matter since there is no legal difference between the two. Both are binding in court. But the fact of the matter is that the word "contract" scares people off and if you have someone sitting on the fence, so to speak, you'll probably lose them at that point.

Have you ever signed a document to buy a home or buy a car? Of course you have. Have you been overwhelmed with the number of sheets of paper you have to either initial or sign? Amazing, isn't it?

I suggest you stay away from long, tedious pages filled with small type and instead opt for a series of "agreement" pages, each one short and to the point. There is something less scary about signing or initializing pages with small amounts of type. It's also easier to get people to quickly initial or sign a whole number of pages than it is to get them to sign one long endless page of super small type. Just the fact that the type is small leads people to "feel" there's something under-handed hidden in all that text.

Keep your documents from looking too legal. Whenever I see a long, contract with ultra small text, I feel the need to call my attorney to preview it first. This is not the sort of feeling you want to instill in your client. Attorneys who show up to preview contracts have a singular objective: to kill the deal. So make it easy and a "safe environment" for your prospect to agree to all you want them to agree to.

Another reason for drawing up simple "agreements" to be initialized or signed is that you can make them as specific and practical as you want. There's no one-size fits all agreement or contract and States have their own requirements that you may have to abide by as well.

Working with a series of agreements feels comfortable and they are easy to create and adapt to the manner and methods you want to use.

Have Your Paperwork Prepared in Advance

Another way you can present yourself in a performance position is to have all of your contracts or agreements already filled out before you arrive. By asking a lot of questions on the phone before you ever agree to go to the property, you'll have much of the information in advance.

Most agreements or contracts have standard statements with blank lines to be filled in. This lets the prospect know that he/she is signing the same type of agreement that all your other clients have signed in the past. You can print off a bunch of agreements in advance, then all you do is fill in the blanks for your client. This is all done at your office before you ever leave to preview the property.

By filling in the paperwork in advance, the prospect sees how organized you are. They see how you're going to save them time by doing much of the work for them. You will, of course, carry identical blank agreements with you so that if a mistake was made or a change is incorporated, you've got the ability to change out the documents on the spot.

Another reason for having the agreement pages filled in already is that it eliminates any fumbling around or delays in getting the client to sign. I've been in situations where the prospect was totally convinced to do business only to have a relative or friend show up and say something negative that killed the whole deal instantly. Plus you don't want to give them extra time for doubt to creep in and cause them to delay. So the moment you know you've brought a prospect to the point of signing your documents, speed the process along by having as little for them to actually do at that moment as possible. The only thing they should have to do is place their initials or signature on the paperwork (and perhaps write out a deposit check).

Can You Pass the Flinch Test?

There is a little test that prospects like to give to every consultant they encounter. It is a test to see if they are confident in the price they presented for their services. Expect it to happen to you. It's called the flinch test. It goes something like this: "Wow! You are 25% higher than your competition."

Business professionals are trained to react with (false) surprise so that they can see if the consultant is confident in the price they have just placed on the table. See it for what it is: Nothing more than a negotiation tactic.

Often times they overstate the price difference so if you do some quick math in your head, you'll see that the differential is bogus – they probably don't even have a quote from a single one of your competitors.

I can recall a time where I was told that I was 50% higher than the competition. My client was comparing my price with a non professional. My client had to do all of the commuting on multiple trips and would receive no service of any kind. He wasn't even comparing apples to apples, which is very unfair. When I pointed out just a few of the major differences, he flinched and I got my price. The whole thing was bogus to begin with.

The key to passing the flinch test is to respond with confidence in your price, and if necessary, point out some obvious differences in what your price includes and what their price would not (assuming you know who your competition is or likely to be and you're acquainted with their services and pricing). If you don't believe you are providing a fair, competitive price for the solution, why are you presenting it in the first place? I would hope your personal integrity would prevent you from doing that.

But here are some responses that will cause you to fail the flinch test. What price were you looking for? I'll rework the numbers and see if I can do better. How about if I take 10% off? (the percentage doesn't matter)

The reason these are failed responses is that they create trust issues with the prospect that weren't there before. They begin to immediately ask themselves: Were you trying to rip them off with the price you presented?
One of two things is true. Either you were trying to rip them off or you believe you provided a fair price. It's one or the other. What other explanation could there be? Some people might claim that they were preparing for a negotiation. For instance, were I to make a proposal to The Donald, I'd have to charge more knowing full well that he will negotiate me down or walk away from me, because he loves to get a lower price from everyone, even if the price is already a fair one.

It is a terrible negotiation strategy to give the appearance that you will drop your price the first moment someone balks. That approach gives the impression that you sought to gouge them from the outset.

Most negotiations end at or near the middle ground. They wanted 50; you wanted 100 and settled at 75. That seems logical. However, if you lower your price early on, the middle ground is lower still. In the same scenario, if you dropped to 80 right off the bat, the middle becomes 65. As I mentioned, you have to manage the negotiation such that the middle is not lower than an acceptable price for your company.

There is a saying, that whoever concedes first loses. And the first time you drop your price you signal to the other party that you'll drop it yet again. And the percentage that you drop it on your first offer, will also signal the amount or percentage that you will drop it on the second round. In any event, you don't want to drop your price immediately under any circumstances and if you do, you want it to be a small increment, not a substantial one. As an example, you want a $5000 fee. The client offers $2000. If you drop your price by $1000, you will signal that you'll come down another $1000 to $3000 total. But if your first discount offer is only $500 (a smaller increment), the client will assume the maximum you'll move down is another $500. So the perceived "meeting place" is $4000 total, not $3000.

Successful consultants have a planned or "canned" response for the flinch test. They don't expect a prospect to respond with excitement about a price. When was the last time you got excited over a price? They anticipate shock and have a process to handle it.

Here are the secrets:

1. **Set expectations upfront and on paper.** Early in the buying process, set the expectation that you are not the low price provider. Say to your client, "To be clear, my company is rarely the low bid. Does that mean that I won't be working with you on this project?" If they say no, you are set for the later phases of the process. If they say yes, at least you haven't invested a ton of time in an account that you won't win. If you are going to lose, lose early and move on to the

next more lucrative project. Let your competition waste their time chasing after small profits.

2. **Don't flinch! Be Prepared.** "I'm not surprised by your reaction. I get that a lot. As I mentioned at the outset, I am rarely the low bidder, but my service can't be matched."

3. **Seek to understand their point of view.** "When you

say that you are shocked by the price, which part is surprising? You've got to understand a prospect's perspective on price before you can comment further or make any adjustments should you decide to do so.

4. **Reinforce your position.** "Since I am rarely the low price provider, what do you think my other clients see that leads them to feel comfortable paying a little bit more to get my services?

To share a little secret, I use the flinch test often when I buy, especially when making major purchases. It's amazing how quickly other people drop their price. I bet I've saved my family 20% across the board for all of our needs just with that test. It's no wonder that professional negotiators use this tactic. I often wonder how many dollars they have lost just because they flinched. How may dollars have you lost because you flinched – especially when you were new in the business?

Time Restraints

Never negotiate when time is of the essence working against you. This puts you at an immediate disadvantage. If you've got a limited time to make a decision one way or another, and you feel highly pressured, walk away from the negotiations. You will hurt your business if you negotiate under pressure.

If you're contemplating taking on a project where time is extremely limited and the other party is claiming "time is of the essence", proceed with extreme caution. Add more to your price and build in extra time in anything you promise. When time is of the essence, on one side or the other, it's amazing how many events can and will happen to challenge the calendar under which you're operating, leaving your business with more exposure than you can manage.

Your Reputation

You know, you don't have to settle for taking baby steps in our industry and waiting over a long period of time to grow your business inch by inch. You can choose this route if you want. And it's better than no route at all.

But you can also choose to *leapfrog* over everyone else in the business, or at least in your local area, by using self-proclamation.

To eliminate competition and its affects on you, you simply commit yourself to operating on a higher level. You do that by claiming to be above others in your field. You don't need someone else's permission to do that. You don't wait for me, or the industry, your newspaper or society at large to proclaim that you're the best or at least someone to be reckoned with. You proclaim it yourself.

As you start to make money, it will be easier for you to make claims about your status. You'll find evidence from your past experiences to support your claims and you will refuse to be intimidated by your competition in the least. Most of the time I ignore what my competition does. I'm not concerned with what they're doing. My philosophy is that they need to be concerned about what I'm going.

And even if this were not true, it's a state of mind. It's a downright refusal to be intimidated by anyone – not your client and not your competition.

It flows from a basic belief in yourself and your true worth. As I've stated many times in my writings, if you don't value what you bring to the table, no one else is going to value it either.

But you'll doubtless have times when your reputation is challenged, either directly or indirectly. And you'll have to make a decision each time as to whether it is serious enough to defend or ignore. But having created your powerful positioning, you want to reach a point beyond being asked who you are. Your goal, then, becomes to be viewed so far ahead of the pack, so far above and beyond the average consultant, that no one questions you or your authority.

When you cannot be intimidated by your prospect, your client or your competition, you'll have arrived. Then you just keep doing what is right and doing what you've disciplined yourself to do, and you'll continue to grow your business until you become wealthy.

Your Business Conduct

Whether you're a service provider or someone else's client, it's always wise to keep a cool head and be polite. This is not only expected of you, but it's just good business practice. There are a certain number of people (and hopefully you're not one of them) who think that a deal should swing their way and only their way. With them it's an "I win – you lose" proposition. They are "soviet style negotiators" (a term not coined by me). They are in it to win all they can win for themselves and they do not care if the other party wins anything at all.

These types of people go on the offensive and are often aggressive, even to the point of being rude and accusatory. They would never think of compromising or making concessions of any kind. They make demands. And if they don't get their demands met in the way they think they should be met, they get angry and make threats and throw tantrums.

Let me tell you that this style of negotiating does not work well for you and will be very bad for your business over the long haul. Yes, you might win a battle here and there, but you will lose the war, because your reputation will be tarnished, perhaps forever.

Every once in a great while, someone will express dissatisfaction in a product I sell. It could be an ebook that they had trouble downloading and viewing. It could be they got angry because they weren't allowed to print off the ebook as they thought they should be able to do. It could be they didn't read the instructions, so when something didn't work as they expected, they got mad.

People invent their own expectations about products and services, which often have little substance in the scheme of things, or have no relevance whatsoever to the other party. No one can control what goes on in the minds of other people. Words are always open to interpretation, which is why they are best put on paper so there is a record of what is being agreed to and that record is available to all parties and is dated and signed.

Even when images accompany words, people will still develop their own private expectations and hopes, and the product or service rendered may or may not live up to these expectations. Sometimes a product or service will far exceed their expectations. Sometimes it will be as expected and sometimes it will fall below the person's expectations. Many people set unrealistic expectations.

But no matter whether the expectations were met, exceeded or not, how you respond is critical and will reflect on you as a business person. You have a right to respond any way you choose to. You have a right to be satisfied or dissatisfied. But that is where your rights end because while you can feel any way you want to feel, when you start to communicate your feelings to the other party, great care should be exercised in the method and manner of your communication.

In my experience, there are two types of communicators regarding expectations.

Some people get hostile. They don't want to accept responsibility for the choices they made on their own and the terms they were willing to abide by when they entered the business transaction. They always, always blame the other party for everything, even when they know in their heart that the fault was all theirs. They often accuse the other party of deceptive practices, even accusing them of doing unlawful acts, such as false advertising and the like.

In most cases, the other party had submitted disclaimers, and their terms and conditions. But the angry receiver did not bother to read these or the terms are suddenly now unacceptable to them for whatever reason they choose. Believe me when I say, it is also not lost on business people that 90% of people who want a refund intended to ask for one before they ever placed the order. They set out to get the product or service for free, at least for a time, and they never had any intention of paying for it when all was said and done.

And once they have made their accusations to the seller or other party, they often make veiled threats (or outright threats) to take some kind of legal action or to make some kind of silly report. This is all geared to try to intimidate or scare the other party into doing what ever they demand of them, whether it be to issue them a full refund (and it's always a "full refund") or to provide them with their own brand of "fair treatment".

Believe it or not, I've had an occasional person demand a refund for a product I've sent them without ever returning the product to me or communicating with me. They throw tantrums, wanting refunds while keeping the product or service.

You will probably run across these types of people from time to time if you're in business for any length of time. So you've got to be aware they are out there.

I've had a handful of people who started out hostile, but after I've pointed out some facts and directed their attention to information they somehow missed, they have come back with sincere apologies. But there inevitably are always those who will never admit that the fault lies with what they assumed or failed to do and go away mad no matter what.

Should the problem stem from something we failed to do, we admit our error and immediately correct the problem, but even then there are people who still remain hostile just because they *can*. In such cases, I'm just as happy to end all association with them as they are to end it with me. That's life. It happens to every business somewhere along the road. Don't be surprised when it happens to you. It's not a matter of *if*, it's a matter of *when*. But don't be alarmed. It is rare if you have taken care to provide outstanding services and products.

Some people remain nice. While they may be dissatisfied with a product or service, they try to be objective and determine in advance whether their expectations were too high or unfairly derived. They wouldn't think of making any accusations against the other party. They are totally willing to accept responsibility for their own decisions in accepting the business transaction in the first place and they will be fair about accepting a resolution.

If they genuinely feel that their expectations were fairly placed and they are dissatisfied, they are wise enough to contact the other party with a polite inquiry to see if the terms can be renegotiated or whether they might return the product for a refund. They don't even necessarily expect a full refund, but a fair one. They ask. They don't demand. And they certainly don't make threats of any kind.

In most cases, their requests are honored, whereas in most cases, when a person is mean spirited, accusatory and threatening, their requests are often denied.

You see, whenever you go on the attack, whether you feel you have a legitimate right to do so or not, you are only going to force the other party to put up a defensive wall and resist you. That's a natural reaction. It's a human reaction.

So all you've initially succeeded in doing is to build a huge wall of resistance and you've greatly increased the odds against getting a resolution to your liking.

There is a saying that goes something like, "You'll get much further with honey than with stings."

I can tell you from personal experience, that the people I deal with who approach me with their concerns in a calm, respectful manner get much farther to their goals than those that attack me (via email or by phone). I will not be bullied and threatened. I will not be intimidated by any client or student. So the absolute worst negotiating tactic one can take with me is to attack me on any level.

On the other hand, I've had a few really smart people, who happened to be dissatisfied for some reason, write me with kindness and gentleness, even compliments. Then in the course of doing that, they have mentioned a frustration or disappointment of some kind and I've jumped through hoops to either remove their frustration or disappointment or have granted them some kind of consideration, be it a full or partial refund or an exchange or replacement.

After all, I'm human and I have feelings too. I'm not some robot or vending machine creating and dispensing products and services. I have earned the right to be respected and approached in a respectful manner. To approach me in any other manner is to be, quite frankly, stupid.

And I'm not alone. You're going to find that everyone feels the same way.

3 - Getting Paid!
How to Deal With the Negative Aspects of Doing Business

Is the Customer Always Right?

There are some people who believe, "The customer is always right (no matter what they claim or how they act)", but that's not reality and just because a customer throws a tantrum, you don't have to cave in and meet their demands. You can if you want to, of course, but it's not mandatory that you do so.

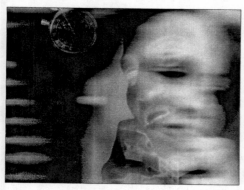 If you're selling an inexpensive product (which requires little time to process) and someone wants a refund, it's probably a good idea to grant their wish. But when you're a consultant, and you've expended serious time and energy in a product or service, the story (in my opinion) is entirely different and you need to stand your ground and abide by your terms and conditions.

The client is NOT always right and the client should not ALWAYS get what they demand, just because they demand it. I can think of few things in business that will demoralize you more than giving into intimidation and threats made to you. It will certainly rob you of your dignity and confidence and ruin your powerful positions you have worked so hard to develop.

In my experience, 9 times out of 10, the customer is flat out wrong or deceptive or untruthful or in error of following directions (or had set out to take advantage of you from the outset). In the vast majority of cases, the client has taken an unfair position, experienced buyer's remorse, set out to take advantage of the other party, or just plain "got it wrong". This is one of the reasons that I require all of my clients be present at the home when I'm working for the following reasons: 1) When I have questions, I want them answered instantly; 2) I want to bond with my client and build a friendship; 3) I want to take my client's "satisfaction temperature" throughout the day so that I know we are both on the same page; 4) I can answer my client's questions instantly and even demonstrate my solutions or suggestions if necessary; 5) I can completely ward off potential problems; 6) My client can see constant progress as the day goes along, sees me and my staff hard at work all day; 7) Adjustments that are needed can be discussed, agreed to, new paper work signed at a moment's notice; 8) I can even send the client on errands if necessary.

Any professional consultant who sends the client out the door while they work is inviting trouble. Yes, I know it's a thrill to surprise them at the end of the day – assuming they like what you have done. But ask yourself: Would I rather surprise my client with my creativity that they might not appreciate or understand and cause a monumental problem as a result **OR** would I rather check with them periodically throughout the day to make sure they are happy and understanding the process and eliminate any and all risk of a problem developing?

To me the answer is a no-brainer. I'll take a problem-free project any day of the week OVER enjoying the opportunity of surprise. There's no better way for a client to really experience a professional home stager at work than by working side by side with one or at least being able to see the progress up close and personal throughout any given day the stager works at the site.

You're going to also discover that men have a bigger problem coping with a drastic change than women. The shock of seeing a drastic change, particularly one made after extensive de-cluttering of the space, can be too overwhelming for some people. That shock alone can set you up for disappointment and criticism.

On a recent staging project, I rearranged the living room furniture to focus on the only focal point in the room, the entertainment center. I actually improved the client's ability to watch TV in the process since they would continue to live in the home until it sold. The room looked 100% better. Later I discovered that the husband, who floated in and out periodically, had expressed displeasure to his wife about the arrangement. He did not like change and did not understand why the furniture had been moved. After it was explained to him that the arrangement was created for potential buyers (and not for his taste) he felt better and relaxed about the new arrangement. Just between you and me, I was astonished that he was unhappy as the new placement was far superior to the old one (and his wife was astonished as well). I can only think then that he has trouble with change of any kind – not surprising for his gender.

If the work had been done without him on the premises and he came home that evening to the room, he would have had no one to explain things to him and he would have "stewed" about it all night and into the following day – or until I would have seen him again. By then he could have become angry about it.

On the web, I'm just stubborn enough (and wise enough) to establish my own terms and conditions of doing business, post them where anyone has access to them, and hold to them until or unless convinced there is good cause to grant an exception.

I made that mistake recently. I offered a sale on my products and services. Every sale has a deadline which could be a few days to a week or two. I announce special sales through my newsletters. After one of my sales closed, a subscriber wrote me a week later and said she wanted to take one of my courses and requested permission to receive the sale price even though the deadline had passed.
For the first time in my business, I decided to grant her the request, and set up a special link for her to use when she placed her order. About a week later she placed the order and received the sale price.

A few weeks later, to my shock, this person anonymously posted online a couple of libelous statements about the course, attacking me personally. Our investigative efforts discovered her true identity.

It seems, without my knowledge, she had acquired a couple of my books elsewhere that are included in the course and was angry that she received duplicate materials. She never mentioned she already had received training from me, either before the sale or after the sale. She also had received training from a seminar somewhere.

Since she already had taken some training from me, and then decided she was happy enough to want to purchase a course, I was stunned to see she had written such scathing comments online, without ever speaking to me or writing to me. Had I known in advance (or even afterwards) that she already had some of my products, I would have been happy to make a substitution for her. But I was never given such a chance.

In the end, not only was I not given a chance to make any adjustments for her prior to the sale nor after the sale, I had broken my own company rule and made an exception for her and gave her a special discounted price after the deadline had passed, which I had never done before and will not do again.

I will never make that mistake again. You will find, unfortunately, that people often do not appreciate the extra mile you go for them, especially when it is free. In my case, the student actually got the duplicated materials for free, because the extra discount she got was more than enough to cover them, but she still decided to go on the offensive.

While I recognize that she wasn't really all that angry about the duplication (but used it as an excuse), and that there was more likely a hidden agenda behind her vindictive actions (which probably had to do with my convictions about the need for merit-based designations in the industry – not fee-based designations), I cannot control what other people choose to do. Nor can you.

I doubt very sincerely that she will survive in business because she is dishonest, unfair in her business practices, prone to taking vindictive actions on the sly and, quite frankly, not a nice person. She even uses the word "diva" as part of her nickname. I guarantee she will repeat her actions in the future with other people and eventually negative feedback will get around, if it hasn't already.

So be wise about breaking your own rules. It could come back to haunt you and should be judiciously extended, if at all. And learn from your mistakes.

But I veered off a bit.

Back to the subject of antagonistic people. Never let anyone intimidate you. If you do, word will get around that you're weak and easily taken advantage of, and this is not good for your reputation. You always want to be fair, but you can't let yourself be trodden underfoot by people who like to intimidate and get preferential treatment at your expense.

This is why I tell you once more: You must pre-determine what you want and what you're willing to do to get what you want. You must also pre-determine what you are NOT willing to do to get what you want, establish your rules and regulations or terms and conditions, put all of it in writing, get signatures and have everything dated. And if you have a website, you should post these requirements and policies on your website as a backup.

Look to Turn a Negative to a Positive

I once was in the process of working at a client's home when in walked the client's sister. I had never met the woman before and had never had any discussions with her about my services. As I was going room by room and rearranging the furniture, the sister began changing the accessories around after I left the room. It took me a little while to figure out what was happening. I had never had this experience before and was reluctant to say anything to my client.

My first solution, which I hoped would work, was to quietly move the accessories back where I had placed them and hope for the best. But then I noticed they got moved once again. Sigh. What to do? Do I speak to the sister? Do I speak to my client? Do I leave things the way the sister wants them? What to do?

Ultimately I decided that I owed it to my client to give her the absolute best, most professional service I had to give, regardless of whether the sister agreed with my ideas or not. So eventually I spoke to my client. I moved things back where I felt they should go and left it to my client to speak to her sister.

Well, I can hear you saying to yourself: Then wouldn't it be better to work when no one is there? In this case, I might agree, but it's such an isolated case I still vote for doing your work while your client is there.

Whenever you encounter a negative situation, deal with it as honestly and courageously as you can. But don't stop there.

Dissect it afterwards, when your emotions have calmed down and you can look at it more objectively. Then see if there was anything you could have done differently to have avoided the situation in the first place. If there is something you can do to prevent it from happening again, take steps to correct the potential problem in the future.

One of my solutions was to make a point of telling my client in advance (and spelling it out in my paperwork as well) that no other persons were allowed in the home while I was working. This means no family dropping by, no neighbors popping in, no children coming home from school to get in the way, no animals milling around inside the house.

In my case, I try to use the situations that I encounter to teach. I've just related a recent experience in hopes you'll learn from it. This not only helps me to deal with the situation, but it helps me to get rid of any negative feelings I might be left with and turn those negative feelings into something positive – something that quite possibly will help someone else in a similar situation. Truth be known, the manual was begun as a result of a key negative experience I have had most recently.

If you can turn negative situations into ways that will make you profits for the rest of your life, so much the better. I have actually gotten great ideas for books to write which came as a direct result of a criticism directed at me or my programs. What someone meant for payback I have turned into profit. So in the end, it is you who profits even more since I fully expect you to take advantage of these warnings and eliminate them from entering your life.

So always look for ways to turn negatives into positives – then move on.

Legal Action Is Always a Possibility

While everything you do and say is hopefully geared to protect your interests, you must know that sooner or later you may have to go to court to get the payment that is due to you. You've got to face reality and not be fearful of it.

You want to do anything and everything possible to avoid lawsuits and avoid the time, energy, aggravation and expense of suing someone. But let's face it. Sometimes they leave you no choice. So you hope for the best but assume the worst; you plan for the best and you plan for the worst. If the worst comes your way, you're neither surprised by it nor caught off guard.

As I said earlier, there's always going to be someone plotting to see how they can get the best of you. So know going in that you cannot guard against every eventuality and in that sense you will always be under-protected.

 Because of this, you want to always build a paper trail of communication between you and your client. And you also want to build a phone trail and/or a fax trail and/or an email trail. Phone records will provide you with a paper trail to phone calls (particularly long distance calls) and fax transmissions. Create a folder in your email account titled the name of your client. When you receive an email from

your prospect or client, save it in a folder you label with the client's name. I cannot stress too much the importance of creating and saving a trail of communication. You never know when you might need it — especially in court.

If you're concerned with somehow being eliminated from the loop (between a client, an agent or a vendor), set up conference calls so that you're always directing the communication between involved parties, keeping them separated and dependent totally on you for information.

If participants in a project can talk to each other independently, you're setting yourself up for agreements and discussions that you know nothing about. That type of communication (which eliminates you) is malignant in nature and spreads rapidly. This is another reason for taking the responsibility to initiate all contact between parties yourself. Remove as much responsibility as possible from everyone else. They will see it as you providing excellent service; you will see it as you protecting your interests.

You should also know that whenever attorneys (yours or theirs) are present prior to a deal closing, they will try to halt it. They are trained to put up a fight — even if they know the fight is useless or even if they believe the terms to be fair. They have to make their clients feel they did something to earn the huge fee they will charge for showing up. So whenever they are brought in by either side, objections will be made. Count on it.

Attorneys probably don't feel justified unless they can kill a deal — at least for awhile. You, on the other hand, are a deal maker. So you want to remain "cool" in the situation. Your attitude should remain positive and you should give the air that there is nothing to be concerned about. You should look on all "problems" the attorneys address as mere "points" to be "managed".

Any time an attorney brings up an issue, you say: "That's a very good point (not problem). I'm glad you brought it up." You would then go on to state the many ways you would handle (not solve) the point (not problem).

You never challenge the attorney. Your whole manner should convey the attitude that the deal WILL CLOSE. Your statements will be all inclusive – in that you assume EVERYONE wants to close the deal.

However, if you see that the attorneys are really messing up the deal for good, you must not let them be the ones to terminate the deal. You must grab back the power by turning to your client and telling your client politely that YOU are turning away from the deal yourself.

It is a rare client who will go against the advice of his/her own attorney, but there are many people who fear losing out altogether when YOU make the move to kill the deal. I don't know what it is, but people just hate to have something taken away from them. There's something in our nature that makes us want what we feel we cannot have.

So if all else fails, stand your ground for what you want from the deal. And if it appears to be falling out on you, announce to your client that YOU are taking the deal off the table. You may just get everything you want in spite of the attorney. And if you end up walking away from the deal, you will retain your dignity in tact. They might not like the terms, but they will respect you as an honorable business person who stands behind the terms you want, even if it means walking away.

When you decide to "pull the plug", you stand up and say something like, "Well, I guess that's it. It looks as if we just can't make this one work." If you ever get to this point, it is time for the seller to decide just how badly he/she wants the deal to go through. Chances are it's the degree of financial desperation on the part of the seller that will be the deciding factor. The more desperate the situation is, the greater chances you have of the seller overriding the attorney and making the deal anyway.

If you, as a professional stager, work hardest on finding and making "workable deals" rather than finding and trying to make "impossible deals", you will be working efficiently and profitably. So remember this: <u>The degree of financial desperation on the part of the seller is the single most important criteria in determining how makable a deal is.</u> If you pick the right person to deal with (someone who has already stuck themselves out on a financial limb), that person will most likely be your ally in the closing stages, even in the face of attorney attempts to block a deal.

Never forget that an attorney is merely a college graduate which a specialized diploma. This diploma grants him/her the right to openly practice intimidation either against you or on your behalf. Desperate sellers probably have not had any opportunity to "train" their attorneys into making sure the deal closes, so the attorney will do what attorneys do – try to find ways to block the progress or kill the deal altogether.

You must make sure any attorney you hire knows what the objective is. You want the attorney to protect your interests – but you also want to close any and all deals that are good for your business and profit margin. You should pre-discuss any points that could be discarded or re-negotiated in the interest of making the deal and which points are deal killers.

But before you go out an hire an attorney, read the next section.

Limit Your Deals to Small Claims Maximums

I actually prefer to work my deals in amounts under the maximum small claims limit in my state. I reside in California where the maximum small claims case is $5000.

Some of you will live in states where the maximum might be $3000 or less. Some of you will live in states where the maximum is a good deal higher than $5000. Check with your local court house to see what the maximum is where you live. Try to keep each deal at or under the maximum amount.

The reason for this is that if you ever have to take a client to court to sue for money owed you, the expense of doing so is considerably less. In small claims cases, you do not use the services of an attorney. You represent the case yourself. This eliminates a whole set of expenses for you whether you win the case or you lose it. Most cases can be brought before a judge for under $100 and if you win the case, the defendant must also pay you back for your court costs. It is typically cheaper to sue an individual than to sue a business.

So you ask: But what if the project is higher than the maximum amount I'm allowed to sue for in my state? What then? The answer is that you break up the deal into smaller increments and you price them out separately into two or more deals (contracts). Each deal is managed separately and should the client refuse to pay one or more of your separate deals, you file one or more lawsuits. Each case is individually adjudicated by a judge and each case gets its own independent judgment. It may be better to file your cases on different days so that the case is heard on a different day and perhaps by a different judge. I'm not sure that matters, but I just throw it out there for consideration.

Let's say you're working on staging a 5,000 square foot home and the total price to do the entire home would be $12,000. That's certainly much higher than you could sue for in one lawsuit in most states should you have problems. So you can manage it two ways.

First, you could require a substantial down payment in advance to begin work on the home. If you had a $5,000 maximum small claims allowance in your state, you would ask for a $7,000 down payment in advance. Then you're fully covered on the remaining balance.

Or you could split up the work on the project in a manner that makes sense, such as putting all the exterior work into one contract and all of the interior work into a second contract. No client would balk at this (probably) and you never disclose to the client the reasons why you are orchestrating two separate contracts. All you need to do is to make sure that each deal does not exceed the maximum amount you could sue for in small claims court. If you still have an overage on one of the deals, then require a deposit in advance on that one contract, leaving a balance that is less than the maximum small claims allowance.

In most cases, breaking a project into two parts should be quite easy for you to do and appear totally logical to the client as well. Of course, you could take it further and do multiple contracts, but then you risk the client asking questions as to the reasoning behind your methods. While you're not doing anything illegal, the less questions the better.

Another way to break up a project into smaller segments is to price all of the labor services into one contract and price all of the rental and purchased products into separate agreements (or break it down further into rental agreement separate from purchased items). This would also appear logical to a client and be acceptable to them with no questions asked.

My only goal here is to get you to minimize your risks. Either a client will pay you with no problems, or a client will try to fudge and escape paying you for all or a portion of your services. By being smart on the front end, you minimize your risks by proportioning them out instead of putting everything into one single contract that has to be adjudicated in one lawsuit, which could potentially leave you unable to collect a portion of what is owed, even though you win the case.

Fortunately most clients are honorable and pay for the services you render without causing you any grief. But the larger a project is, the greater are the chances that a fly in the ointment will appear. You never want to wind up in court (small claims or otherwise). But if you do have problems, you want to give yourself the best possible chance of getting all the money owed to you with the least amount of struggle.

Collecting the Data You Might Need

It's one thing to sue a small business or to sue a corporation in a small claims case. It has been my experience that it is easier to collect money owed to you if you must sue a corporation. While the fees to sue a corporation or a business are higher than the fees to sue an individual, sometimes it can be more difficult to collect from an individual.

First of all, if you are discussing a large, time consuming project for a homeowner and the homeowner is self employed, then you might have more trouble collecting your judgment after you win your case. The reason is that if the client owns their own business, chances are they do not receive a salary, so there are no wages you can attach.

It would therefore behoove you to find out as much information on the front end as you can that could be very useful to you in the event you ever had to sue your client.

So be sure to include spaces in your contract to quietly get that information. Here are some obvious bits of personal information that I recommend you include and you might talk to your attorney to see if you need anything else:

- Place of Employment
- Employer's Street Address and City
- Name of Supervisor
- Employer's Phone Number and Extension
- No. of Years Worked
- Auto License Number
- Social Security Number
- Name of Bank and Address
- Bank Account Numbers

Collect the same information from the spouse:
- Spouse's Place of Employment
- Spouse's Employer's Address
- Spouse's Supervisor
- Spouse's Employer's Phone Number and Extension
- Spouse's No. of Years Worked
- Spouse's Auto License Number
- Spouse's Social Security Number
- Name of Bank and Address
- Bank Account Numbers

Other information that could be valuable:
- Nearest relative
- Nearest person to contact in an emergency
- 3 credit references
- 1 personal reference (or more if you want)

Assuming you win your court case, the defendant will have the opportunity to appeal the ruling. Here in California, a defendant can appeal the ruling within 30 days and the case is kicked up to superior court for another judge to hear.

After you win that case as well, you are then given a final judgment which is good for 10 years and is renewable. The unfortunate part about court cases (besides the costs and time involved) is that the court offers only a few ways to help you actually collect the money owed you.

When suing a client who works for a company, you can have their wages attached if they don't pay you. It involves filing documents with the court and letting the court serve the employer. The amount of the ruling and all of the court costs are then deducted out of your client's wages and sent to you. If your client does not work for a business or corporation or you do not know where they work, it becomes much more difficult to extract the money owed to you.

Finding out the critical information you will need to attach wages is very difficult after a situation has gone awry and so for this reason it is best to garner important information on the front end. I'm sure you've been to a doctor within the past couple of years and had to fill out a form that asks you for all sorts of information of this nature. They want to be sure they have recourse should you not pay your bill.

If a client ever baulks at giving you this type of information, just explain to them that it is company policy to collect it just as their own doctor would do. Anyone who has ever been to the doctor, filled out a credit application, purchased an auto loan or other type of contract knows full well that prudent companies collect extra information for these purposes.

If your client is self-employed I recommend you collect a larger deposit if you're concerned about getting paid.

Don't be surprised if you get a call the day before the court date offering you a settlement. Settlement offers are generally well below the amount you are suing for and you should be prepared for giving an answer. If you're willing to settle, pre-determine what your bottom figure would be and stick to it. Don't forget to factor in the costs you will have paid out to file the lawsuit in the first place, plus the time involved in having to go to court to file the paperwork and in having the client served with the summons.

I once received a call the day before by my client's attorney offering me a ridiculous amount of money to settle at the last minute. I refused. The attorney then offered to pay the full amount and wanted me to call the court and inform them right then that the suit had been settled. I refused to do so until I had payment in my hand. So then the attorney invited me to drive over to his office to pick up a check. I refused to leave my office and told him it was up to him to see that the money got delivered to me that day. Within a few hours a courier showed up with the money.

You won't be able to count on this type of offer, but you should be prepared to receive a last minute offer in case one does come your way. If the call comes to you from an attorney, don't feel intimidated. I promise you that the client does not want to pay a high priced attorney to represent them in court, even if an attorney was allowed. It will be in their best interest to settle the case without appearing in court. By knowing this, you'll be in the driver's seat.

Close Your Deals as Soon as Possible

The longer your prospect goes trying to make a decision, the less likely it will be that you will get the project. This is why it is important to assume control of every conversation and meeting so that you can move your prospect into making the deal as soon as possible. When people take time to "think about it", they forget all of the great points you've made; your visuals dim in their memories. They start to doubt their initial impressions. Circumstances always seem to get in the way.

You are committed naturally to getting hired and getting paid. Your prospect will naturally be committed to stalling on both issues.

For this reason, try to make all your submissions in person, not by email, not by mail. Unless you send mail by certified or registered mail, you'll never know if the party received it. And you won't have any proof either. You'll always want to send documents by certified mail <u>after</u> you get a signature, to strengthen your paper trail, but those are duplicate documents to what you gave them in person.

Email, FAX and mailed documents are impersonal. Email might not reach them or might get deleted without ever being read. Mail can get lost or, at best, takes extra days to arrive. When dealing with homeowners, they aren't likely to have a FAX at home unless they have a home business.

But even more than that, when getting signatures, it is much harder for people to say "no" to your face. You can get with the person quickly, reassure them they are making a great decision, get the signature sealed on a document quickly and bond with your new client in ways you can never do through email, FAX or by mail.

When it comes to business deals, the soon the better. Strike while the iron is hot. You never know when by being one minute sooner, one hour sooner, one day earlier, one week earlier, you could effect the difference between making and not making a deal.

Always Be the Last to Leave

If you are meeting with multiple parties in a meeting at a location that is not your office, always be the first to arrive and the last to leave. You don't want people having discussions that involve you before you arrive and you certainly don't want them having discussions without you after the meeting ends.

If you are trying to protect your interests and prevent other parties from forming relationships between themselves separate from you, then make arrangement to pick up the other party and go together to the meeting. This also gives you control over that person's conversations until you have delivered them back home.

You will be viewed in any case as providing outstanding service, but in reality you will also be protecting your own interests.

In the home staging business, you're usually working in concert with a real estate agent as well as the home owner, so keeping the lines of communication open and running through you as much as possible is imperative.

Always Tell the Truth

You'd think I wouldn't have to include a section on the subject of truth vs. lying. But it seems to be an increasing problem in all facets of business and life. We've got politicians who lie; we've got attorneys who lie; we've got professional athletes who lie; we've got corporate executives who lie; we've got spouses and children who lie.

And it doesn't seem to matter if they are in a court of law or not – people still tell lies or get their high-priced attorneys to distort the truth. Just think of the mess in the Casey Anthony situation (the Florida 19-year-old who claims her daughter, Caylee, was kidnapped by a babysitter and didn't report her missing for over 30 days, then lied continuously to police, parents and others about the situation).

Lying may get you out of trouble in the short term, but it inevitably will catch up with you in the long term. And you can almost always tell when someone is lying because their statements are generalities rather than specifics; their stories keep changing as well. When a person is telling the truth, the story never changes because the truth is the truth and facts are facts.

This is another reason why it is so important for you to memorialize all of your business agreements in writing. You want a paper trail to document all of your agreements and the terms of such agreements, including the dates. This is to make sure you and your client are "on the same page" but also to protect all parties involved in case of a dispute down the road.

My advice is to quickly admit to a fault if you have made one. Don't lie about it. Advise your clients honestly on the front end and make a written record of it. If it turns up you made a mistake, admit it. Don't hide it. Don't falsify any records or make false claims. It will not serve you in the end and as a matter of fact, it could harm your reputation and your business name. Many people have had to close their business down because they not only got caught doing something illegal, but they tried to hide the fact after they were discovered and it ultimately brought their business to total ruin.

The truth is easy to tell.
The truth is easy to remember.
The truth is the right path to follow.

You'd be surprised how many people are forgiving and forgetting when you own up to your mistakes right away and apologize for them. On occasion we make mistakes too. Everyone does now and again. That is human. We rectify our mistakes promptly, make refunds where appropriate, correct what needs correcting and own up to our failures.

I've even found it really good to joke about being forgetful, or being a bonehead or some other light-hearted self-deprecating description. People appreciate you for your honesty and willingness to admit you're not perfect. In a world full of people who don't want to accept responsibility for anything they do incorrectly, it's refreshing to run across someone who accepts responsibility.

This is how you should conduct business at all times. I guarantee you, even if it stings a bit in your wallet or ego, it will be far less painful to admit your faults right away than to stall, lie or cheat. Just ask Marion Jones or some of the other professional athletes caught for steroids. Ask John Edwards. Ask Casey Anthony (well, maybe not).

Immediate acceptance of responsibility will ensure your business will continue. But if you lie, you may just lose your business or your reputation.

It's All About Compensation – Not Deals

Remember, the goal is to get compensated for work you have done. Landing a deal is only the first step. You've got to execute the work in a satisfactory manner and you've got to make sure you get paid. Until you have been fully paid, you are in a vulnerable position and there is no room for celebration – not yet.

Once you have a signed contract, you must try to execute your part of the contract as quickly and as efficiently as possible. The more time that transpires, the more you open yourself up to the seller's natural tendency (at some point) to look for ways to challenge the deal.

The less desperate the seller is to get the home staged and on the market, the more "staying power" he/she has. Wealthy people have staying power because they have lots of money. They use their wealth to bluff and intimidate you. They know they can get away with their bluff because they have the money to hold out for what they want to get. You probably will not be in that position and this puts you automatically into a vulnerable spot. So you'll have to create your own staying power built on something other than wealth. You'll have to anticipate that a bluff might come along, even after the paperwork is signed. You'll have to muster up your own set of "guts" and stand your ground no matter what. You'll have to draw your own imaginary line in the sand. The imaginary line will act for you as a fortress: Beyond this line there is no intimidation. Beyond this line there is no bluff allowed.

This is the power of getting a healthy percentage of your fee up front in the way of a non-refundable deposit. When I had a new roof put on my home, my contractor was prevented by law from asking for more than 10% down payment. That's because he works in a regulated industry. While I have never had any problem asking for a higher percentage for my work (as much as 50%), you'll have to test this out in your own area to see what percentage you can command.

Whenever I sell a product, I always ask for my full cost minimum to be paid to me in advance. In this manner, should a client back out of a deal (for whatever reason) and should I be unable to get any further compensation, I at least have the product completely paid for by the client. I may be stuck with it – but at least it didn't cost me anything. So I recommend you work hard to protect yourself from spending any money before getting paid by the client. In most cases, however, I demand full pre-payment – and I get it too. I've found that most people will give you what you ask for, especially if it is in writing. They tend to think the terms are non-negotiable if they are in writing.

So I cannot emphasize it enough. Once you have a signed contract, where money is still owed to you, get to work immediately. We all know how notorious the home improvement industry is with contractors taking on more work than they can handle and making clients furious with their on-again off-again practices. This is why it is so important for you to choose reliable vendors to manage certain aspects of your services. In the end, it's your reputation on the line and clients don't want to hear about your problems or predicaments, no matter how legitimate they are.

They want the project to run smoothly and on time. If you hire sub contractors to handle a portion of the project, you are still the one the client will blame if things go wrong. So you've got to be on top of the situation and the project at all times.

Make sure when you promise the timing on certain aspects of a project that you build in enough lead time to accomplish the tasks on time. Any and all failed completion dates will work against you in the client's mind and give them ammunition to try to keep from paying a portion or the remainder of the contract.

Whenever possible, do all the work yourself. You KNOW you're reliable. But when it isn't possible to do it all yourself, hire reliable people who do quality work, even if they charge you a higher fee. This is paramount to the success of your business and the ability to get those all important referrals when everything is said and done.

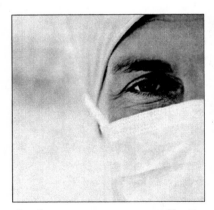

I don't know of a faster way to suffer from the disease called "stagingdectomy".

Stagingdectomy is the surgical removal of your fee for services by the seller. It happens to real estate agents all the time who have not protected themselves properly when it comes to their commissions. It can happen to the home stager as well. It most certainly increases in frequency if you do not have signed documents of your "deal" and have not used certified mail to further document your paper trail.

There are some people who will, after the fact, look for ways to scoot out of certain provisions you've agreed to in the contract. Thankfully it doesn't happen all the time or even half the time, but it can happen to you at any time, so you must be prepared for it and not caught off guard.

One common tactic used by sellers is to whine and moan about how much money they have already sunk into the property that makes it extremely difficult to pay out more money. Or another tactic might be to complain about how much time has already been wasted causing them to pay two mortgage payments, depleting their reserves dramatically. Some people will agree to anything thinking they can get the promised amounts adjusted after the fact – naturally adjusted to their enrichment, not yours. Another strategy is for the seller to come across as a really "nice" person, as a very docile person. This type of strategy has the person scratching their head and looking confused. This strategy is geared to make you relax and view them as someone who doesn't pose any threats. They might even speak with a thick accent, making you think they don't know what's going on. Don't be fooled by overly nice people or people with thick accents.

They might even be audacious enough to suggest to you that you "write this one off as experience", giving them a financial break you had not intended to give. Suggestions like these usually include false promises of "more work" in the future or right around the corner. Or they may promise a bevy of referrals in exchange for a price adjustment in their favor.

Stand your ground.

Promises are not worth the paper they are written on and certainly not worth anything at all when spoken. These are all tactics sellers pull on stagers they deal with and you've got to see through them for what they are.

When they are all through pleading their sudden "hardship" case, you turn the tables on them by saying something like, "Well, I'd love to make an adjustment in your favor, really I would, but I just can't. I've got 5 mouths to feed of my own, vendors to pay and obligations I refuse to dishonor no matter how hard it is for me to keep my word. My word is gold to them and my word is gold to you. We need to keep the contract as it was originally set up."

Never engage in hostile discussions, but plead your own hardship case and the fact that you uphold the agreements you make to everyone. This in itself should end the matter without further discussion.

One Last Protective Strategy

This strategy is risky as it might get you eliminated from consideration. But there may be times when you should overbid a project with the sole goal of protecting yourself from situations that can be problematic. For instance, you should pad your expenses and pad your lead time you use to calculate your charges.

But there could be certain situations where it is very advantageous to overly pad your fee so that when things go wrong you have a drop back amount you can go to that will still get you your usual fee.

If you really want to take on a project, but you anticipate in advance there will be problems, or you're not that sure about the total honesty and integrity of your client (but you want the project anyway), then consider charging an excessive fee way beyond your normal fee.

This gives you automatic wiggle room if your suspicions turn out to be correct. It's kind of like giving your self an insurance policy against not getting paid. If nothing negative happens, you make an extra profit, but if you have to concede an adjusted amount down the road, you'll be giving up the bonus profit, not your real profit.

I would only do this if I felt the profit potential outweighed my misgivings by a wide gap. Otherwise I would pass up the project in the first place. So it's a judgment call you'll have to make.

Learn to Face Reality

Your goal in business is to face reality – even when that reality is painful. When you lose money in the stock market or the FOREX market, it is painful and there is always something inside you that tempts you to hang in a little longer in the hopes of rectifying the situation. Giving into that temptation is letting your emotions control your decision making abilities. It is a dangerous thing to do in the stock market, even riskier in the FOREX market, and risky to do in your staging business as well.

Reality is not how you wish things to be. Nor is it the way things appear to be. Reality is the way things actually ARE. For many people, as I'm sure you're aware, facing reality has meant walking away from the home they purchased. For others it has meant walking away from a loss of another sort.

You have to learn how to use reality to benefit you rather than allowing reality to work against you. By focusing totally on the necessity of getting paid, your reality will surely begin to work in your favor. Home staging is not an end in itself; home staging is merely the means to receiving income (profit). Landing projects is pretty meaningless unless you get paid for your time, your effort and your expertise. I'd rather not have a project at all than to be paid less than I feel is fair. And not being paid at all is a curse to be avoided at all cost.

Yes, with every project you will gain experience and you will have additional pictures and stories. But the name of the game is profit – not experience.

Admire your prospects and clients all you want. But that doesn't mean you should work for free or below what you want or need to make. When it comes to running your business, do what is in your *best* interest when it comes to determining compensation. Do not make the mistake of thinking or assuming that if you do a good job, you'll get what you deserve.

Looking out for your own interests is not a conflict of interest. It's a given that you will do a good job, that you will do the best job you are capable of doing. Right? You better say "yes".

All I'm saying is that you must make sure you get paid for the great service you render. You have a right to be compensated for a great performance and never let anyone intimidate you into believing otherwise.

Sometimes Tough Love is Required

Today I received a phone call from a Diamond trainee who is on the verge of completing her Certification requirements. She related a story of working with a widow and 14 –year-old daughter who were struggling emotionally with the aftermath of the death of the husband and father. She told me about how much friction existed between the mother and daughter, and how the mother wanted to hang on to collectible dolls in the daughter's room that the daughter was ready to pack away. When a verbal fight ensued between the mother and daughter, the stager/re-designer excused herself so as not to be caught in the middle.

Sometimes you'll find yourself in the middle of circumstances and emotions that are so deep and volatile you wind up in the middle if you're not careful. In most cases it's best to remain as neutral as possible and exit the situation temporarily until calmer emotions prevail again.

But you also have to recognize that you may be the calm in the storm and that your presence and loving suggestions can ease tensions and help mightily in the situation.

I once had a client that came as a result of a corporate art installation I did. She worked in personnel for the corporation and was married to a driver for a well known shipping company. They fought all the time. I was never in a room with the two of them without a verbal fist-a-cuffs starting up. The wife even told me once they have a love/hate relationship.

The husband, who knew nothing about design or staging, belittled the wife constantly, who actually had some good ideas and wanted to learn from me. To make matters worse, their personal taste on décor was quite different.

So it became my task to find a common ground on which to build in the hopes of making both of them happy and content. I remember well standing there in silence as the two of them argued, waiting for one or the other to ask me my opinion.

It's a tricky place to be in, but you must remember that you are the professional and they look to you to solve the dilemma.

So gently and as kindly as possible, you need to give the advice that you feel is best, trying at all times to get them to compromise. Ways to do that are to suggest the husband's ideas be incorporated into one room while the wife's be incorporated into another room.

I have also had times when I've simply said, "I don't recommend we go in either of those directions. Here's what I recommend we do instead." Somehow taking the matter out of both of their hands and taking over completely is the best route. Then neither party can claim victory over the other one and sometimes all that is happening is a "power game".

I think in these types of situations you'll have to draw down on your training and expertise, and your experience in other situations, and make the recommendations you feel are best, no matter if you agree or disagree with either party.

You are being paid to create an environment that pleases the most potential **buyers** possible – not to please the husband or the wife. They are the sellers, not the potential buyers.

So you need to gingerly explain the goals to both of them, calm them down and move on from there. In most cases, they will relax and let you take over. Then good, bad or indifferent, they can blame you if things don't work out as anticipated. That's why you're getting paid after all.

If you come up against a client that adamantly refuses to take your advice, exclaim to them, "Ok, that's fine. We'll do it your way, but under NO circumstances are you ever to tell anyone that I was your stager!"

The shock of a statement like that will probably make them take a step back and reassess their stance. It should rarely happen but you could inadvertently find yourself trying to satisfy a highly opinionated, truly ignorant client. I did once when I was young and inexperienced in my early days in the business and not as careful in analyzing a situation as I am today.

This is why it is so important to ask a lot of questions first and get to know your potential client BEFORE you agree to take on the project. As you gain experience and clout, you'll reach a point where you won't even hesitate to ask the prospect early on if they have the temperament to lay all of the decisions at your feet or whether they see themselves as wanting to keep control over the project irregardless of what anyone else thinks.

It's a very interesting type of question to ask on the front end and you'll find out rather quickly about the opinions the wife has of the husband and how he feels about her. If you see red flags, pass on the project. Life is too short to deliberately place yourself in a tempest.

On the other hand, if you're dealing with someone going through grief over the loss of a child or parent or spouse, you just may find this client brings you the most happiness you'll ever experience.

It is in the challenges of this type of client that you'll be able to minister to them at a deep emotional level, not just the surface level. You just may have a chance to affect their lives in a substantial way that transcends making profit.

And in a situation like this, you'll be at your best!

4 - Getting Paid!
How to Make Sure You Excel at What You Do

More Ideas, Aids and Tools

You probably already know the standard tricks of the trade, which I've expounded on previously in other publications, but here are a few ideas you may not have thought about or have forgotten.

Use creative fabrics and ideas to help define an area. For instance, let's say you need to gently block off an area or define a work area, a play area, a conversational pit, an entry.

Use string curtains for an unusual effect that will really make your projects stand out from all others.

Use dramatic large art to create a strong focal point and make a major statement.

Create extra drama and an unforgettable visit using minimalism. This art treatment would be more effective hung lower, but you get the idea.

Remember, the whole idea when staging a home is to make the home stand out in the minds and hearts of all the potential buyers. Since buyers will be looking at several properties over a period of time, you've got to do what it takes to help that home stand out in their minds – and yes, even motivate them to place an offer right away for fear they will lose the opportunity to buy the home.

Never mess with a great view (in spite of the telephone poles). If you must, then use sheers.

Use seating and area rugs to define rooms within great rooms. But don't make the mistake of placing a coffee table so far removed from the sofa that it is unusable (as shown here). Just because a room is extra large, don't spread the furnishings out to "fill" it. Keep the vignettes "tight" and functional.

Go all out on draperies to make a grand statement if the room really requires strength in one part of the room. Not necessarily recommended for staging, but when redesigning, that's another matter.

You can even add a special element to an outdoor patio by hanging some sheer drapes, even if you do so sparingly, the buyer's will love the look and get inspired.

Cut down on a messy back yard or overly large back yard by defining the space with a movable gazebo. They aren't that expensive to have at least one as a prop to rent out.

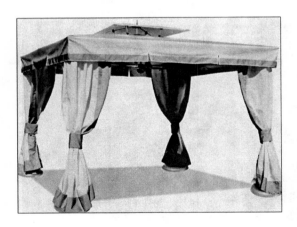

When improving the front or back yard, look for ways to use landscape elements that require no up-keep. You aren't going to know how long that home will remain on the market, and the less up-keep the owner has to worry about the better. Add some rocks and residential boulders to the plan.

Small, portable indoor fountains are easily placed in important areas. Have the owner or agent turn them on during an open house. Make sure that the area surrounding the fountain is well protected against over spray.

You can purchase many different styles of indoor fountains. The sound of trickling water is a peaceful sound to most people and there's no harm in adding "sound" to the atmosphere.

Choose soft, soothing music to add to the allure. Take easy listening music from several CDs and burn to a single long playing CD that can provide hours and hours of enjoyable background music. Set the player on loop so it will play the CD or tape over and over again.

Buy music books or sheet music and place in a room, on a table, on the piano to suggest a music room or practice area.

Bring in that workout machine you quit using years ago and rent it as one of your props.

Find a place indoors or outdoors for a couple of pillars. Place pottery or plants on top for an unusual look.

Try a decorative ladder for a great effect.

Leave it plain like this or drape blankets or throws on it (sparingly, of course).

If any of your props are for sale, attach small sales tags with your business card inserted. It acts like advertising while giving the pricing details about the product.

An easy, portable wall ornament that is also light weight is the large Asian fan. Since it is so different from what you ordinarily see on a wall in place of framed artwork, it will help get that room remembered. Imagine buyers referring to the room as, "You remember – the room with the large oriental fan." Or "You remember the house - the one with the neat ladder leaning up against the wall in the family room."

Leave small containers of potpourri in the rooms to minimize foul odors after you have left the home.

When the scent begins to fade, you can spruce it up with more fragrant oils. Just stirring the mix gets scents buried on the bottom out into the air.

Get a supply of stick up lights. You can put them just about anywhere you need extra light for your project. Use them while you're working; leave them for buyers to use afterwards. Of course, you charge for them. They also make great thank you gifts after the project is done and you've *been paid.*

There are also the dot-it lights that are flat and can be stuck to most surfaces. The light only shines straight from the bulb, so they do not illuminate the same as a light bulb.

But the dot lights are great for adding just a bit of light in a specific area. You can use them on the floor as "up-lights" to cast shadows on a wall. They are safe and long lasting too.

Never forget the power of a great area rug. You might not want to have an all white rug like this one, but I just want you to see the impact and statement such a rug can make on a dark, hard floor. It just makes you want to lie down on it, don't you agree? Even in a black and white photo, it's a spectacular statement.

Room dividers can also be very handy props to have, particularly in neutral colors. Of course one is familiar with the Asian shoji type dividers, but those can be too style specific. Go for ones that will be workable in just about any type of style like this one.

I've said before that repetition of elements creates rhythm and you get more power in your decorating when you group like-kinds together. That goes for plants as well as furniture and accessories.

Candles, of course, are one of the decorating favorites. Remember to group them for best results. The heights should vary and drop in increments of about 1/3rd as you see pictured here.

You can purchase beautiful candle sets from places like Bed, Bath and Beyond, any department store or over the internet. Just do a search on the phrase "candle sets" and you'll see plenty of resources. They are quite inexpensive and look fabulous. Keep your eyes peeled for sales.

Have some custom plaques made to include your name, your business name, your phone or email address and the fact that the home was staged by you. Place at least one plaque in each home you stage as a way to draw special attention to your business cards, which you will also place close by.

You can order plaques over the internet or visit your local awards and trophies retailer to have them made. Do you think this will make a quality statement for you when you're not around?

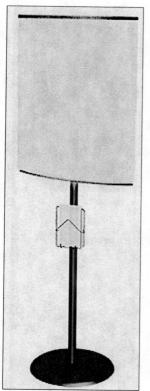

You should also purchase outdoor signage that can be stuck in the lawn or dirt in the front yard, especially during an open house. It alerts everyone entering and leaving that you were the stager and how to get a hold of you. Mention that you also provide interior redesign services for all buyers, both of this property and any other property they may visit during their hunt.

Again there are some really inexpensive signs you can get but remember these act just like calling cards. My advice is to spend a little more and get something with a little style. It will not only draw more attention to your sign's message, it will subtly imply that you are a quality business. Best placed where there is no wind.

This stand holds pictures of a beautiful woman, but what if it held some of your before and after pictures blown up to fit? This type of stand will display up to 6 pictures or a flyer or some testimonial pages. Each display element can be flipped to the other side, making it quite versatile, interesting and something that will definitely attract attention.

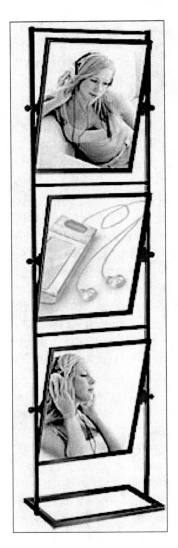

There are always ways to get the message out in a subtle manner or a bold manner (see example above). Consider having a custom sign made to lean up against a wall inside a home. However, if it is quite large, put it in a discreet place. The idea is for people to notice that you staged the home, but you don't ever want to "upstage" the home with your advertising.

During the holidays (or during slower times of the year) offer special discounts on your services to potential buyers, prospects and former clients. You can easily leave many "surprise gift tags" around a home that will appeal to buyers. You can also mail them out in envelopes or make them the size of a postcard and use as a self mailer.

Be sure to include your business card glued or stapled to the back. Leave plenty so that buyers will feel free to take one or several. You don't care how many they take, so long as they eventually use them. Be sure to put a deadline date to ensure they are acted upon right away. You don't want someone asking for their discounted price for a service during a time of the year when you're swamped.

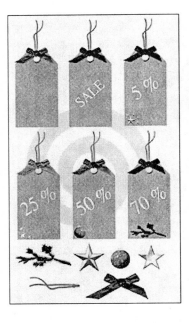

You can even make beautiful gift bags out of holiday wrapping paper as shown here. Sprinkle these through the home during an open house or just leave some behind when you're all done.

Take plain wrapping paper that is color coordinated with the home or your business logo, and make your paper bags.

Attach a before and after picture of the home you just staged on the outside of the bag. (This is an elaborate gift bag made professionally, which you could use as a thank you gift to your client after the staging project is done – and you've gotten paid.)

Do simple ones to use for advertising purposes, however. Include your card and a gift certificate for services on the inside. These are quite easy to make when you're watching television and will go a long way to helping you market your services to "prime" targets, not just anyone.

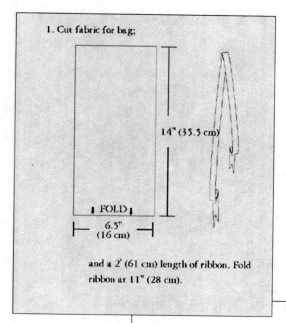

1. Cut fabric for bag:

14" (35.5 cm)

FOLD

6.5"
(16 cm)

and a 2' (61 cm) length of ribbon. Fold
ribbon at 11" (28 cm).

Here's a little pattern
for making gift bags
out of fabric.

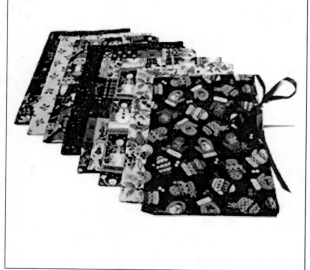

Don't go to elaborate lengths to make these types of
promotional products and then give them out to just any
one. No, you only want to put these into the hands of people
who are right then and there strong potential clients, either
for a redesign appointment or for a staging project.

This is how you target the best and most prime candidates for your services.

Visit the dollar stores in your area and look for cheap toys, such as a little wagon or truck or anything you think will relate to the home. Use these as "gift baskets" when you're done with a project.

Always, always include a business card or a card asking for the client's referrals. These will get you remembered favorably, and that is one of the key elements to getting referrals.

Use humor to create a lasting, memorable message on a door hanger.

Leave the door hanger on the inside of the front door, so that as buyers leave the premises it will be the last thing they see. Hopefully you leave them laughing and carrying fond memories of their experience visiting the home that you have staged.

These examples are from the hotel industry, but you can create your own and have them made up.

Be sure and include your contact information discreetly on the front (not the back) because you don't want people being tempted to take the door hanger with them.

Put a serious door hanger on the front door outside announcing that the home has been staged by you.

Be sure to leave one on the inside door of the bathrooms so that if a buyer uses the toilet they will have something of interest, and humor, to occupy them during that time. Again, be sure your contact information is noticeably on the front if you don't want them to be taken.

If you're using them for advertising and you want people to take them, then put your contact information on the back or make it small enough so that people will still enjoy having your product in their home for any length of time.

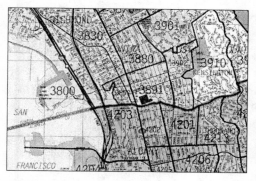 If you don't have a Global Positioning System in your car to help you navigate from home to your appointments, get a Thomas Brothers map for your area. You should find them at any office supply store and major department stores and auto parts stores. Thomas Brothers makes quality maps that are divided into categories to help

you locate an address on the page where it appears. Keep the map in your glove compartment or under your seat where the sun cannot deteriorate it. This will preserve the life of the map.

You'll find very quickly that your automobile might wind up as an additional office. So it's a good idea to start out well organized.

There are many different types of organizers. Some sit on the seat like this one, some hang on the back of seats. Choose the kind that fits your business style and the available room you have in your auto.

Be sure to keep an accurate log of your mileage. Your operating costs (or a percentage of your overall auto expenses), plus depreciation, are all tax deductible. Don't neglect to record all mileage on business trips, including trips to the bank and post office.

When creating your website and/or materials, you can capture your own images with your own digital or traditional camera. But you can also purchase what's called "stock images" from companies on the internet. Most offer package deals and you buy "credits". Each download then costs you so many credits. One such popular stock image seller is www.istockphoto.com.

While these are generic images, you can sprinkle them in your literature to help demonstrate a concept or idea or to just convey in a flash that your business is about interior design services.

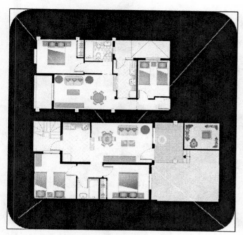

Be sure to purchase "vectored" images unless they are photographs. These are digital images that will not deteriorate in quality, whether the image is reproduced small or large. When using images on a website, it is best to display them in a smaller file size to reduce the download time. But often that makes the finer details unreadable. A vectored image will reduce that deterioration and keep a reasonably good representation no matter what size it is.

This is an example of a whimsical image from istockphoto.com. They have a large variety of images and they continuously offer new ones.

There are, of course, a wide number of companies that provide images for your use. Some are free to download

and others require a fee and do have restrictions, so check those out before you buy.

Most people think of companies such as www.wallwords.com or www.uppercaseliving.com as places to order phrases and words to be transferred to the walls of the home. And yes, this is the primary reason one would visit sites like these. But you should be thinking like an entrepreneur, always on the lookout for a great way to advertise your business. What if you had something custom designed, with your logo or without it, but that included your name, phone number and email address, and instead of transferring it to a wall, you transferred it to archival paper, had it framed and you hung your message somewhere in the home you've just staged, to be retrieved later after the house sells? You could actually transfer the message to anything sturdy and preferably light weight, but it's a quick way to create something that looks fabulous for very little investment. So don't limit the use of wall words and phrases to the obvious usage. Think outside the box and see what you can come up with.

Use your samples and swatches to create a Color Board for your client if you're also offering other products, such as flooring, carpeting, window treatments, paint, wallpaper, seating fabrics and so forth. See examples of 2 color boards.

Paint samples from the local paint store have been fanned out to show how the various colors will blend together. Sometimes a sample of fabric will be too big for the board, but you've got to incorporate it somehow. A photo of the room is included as well, so that a client clearly knows the colors chosen for any given room in the home.

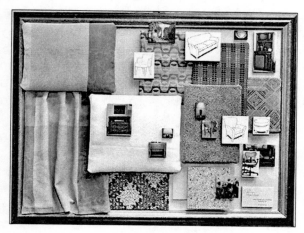

A fan deck, which you can get from your local paint store for a small fee is a must have if you are specifying paint selections for your clients. Look for paint brands of quality and if you're not sure, ask a sales associate at the store to make recommendations to you.

I like Behr Paints (available at Home Depot) but their brand is not carried at all stores. And many paint companies only sell their house brand.

Take note. Most fan decks put all of the yellow hues, red hues and green hues into the warm side of the fan. They put the blue hues and purple hues into the cool 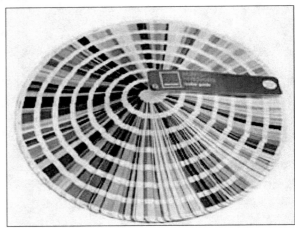 side. Truth be told, there is a warm and a cool version of every color. Warm colors have extra amounts of yellow pigment in them. Cool colors have extra amounts of blue pigment in them. So you can never take a specific color family and designate it as being purely warm or purely cool. So don't rely on the fan deck to tell you one way or another.

Here is a list in alphabetical order of some of the top paint companies in the United States:

3M
- Ace Hardware
- Akzo Nobel
- Altana Group
- Ameron International
- Arch Chemicals
- Asian Paints
- BASF
- Becker Group
- Benjamin Moore
- Behr Paint
- Bona Kemi
- Chugoku Marine Paints
- Cloverdale Paint
- COMEX Group
- Corimon
- Diamond-Vogel Paints
- Dunn-Edwards
- DuPont
- Duron Paint & Wallcoverings

- Ferro
- Hempel
- H B Fuller
- ICI Paints
- Jotun
- Kelly-Moore Paints
- Lord
- MAB Paints
- PPG Industries
- Professional Paint
- Red Spot Paint and Varnish
- Renner-Herrmann
- Rinol
- Rodda Paint
- Rohm and Haas
- RPM International
- Sherwin-Williams
- Sico
- SigmaKalon
- Sika Group
- Smiland Paint
- Stahl International
- Sto Group
- Tigerwerk
- Total
- Tnemec
- Truserv
- Valspar
- Wattyl

Here are some of the most common picture hanging hooks.
You can buy them at any home improvement store or art
gallery.

The nice thing about these types of hooks is that the nails have a head on them, which keeps them from working their way into the wall over time.

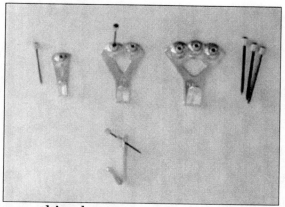

Two of the hooks require 2-3 nails, which provides greater protection, especially if you live in earthquake country as I do.

If you're going into drywall where there is little support and you want to hang something heavy, you need to use anchor bolts in the holes.

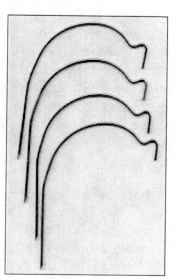

These hooks, on the other hand, are perfect for drywall. You make a small hole in the drywall, push the long end through the hole, turn the hook so that it points up in the front and back, and hang your picture.

When you want to remove the picture, simply turn the hook and pull it out. It leaves a small hole which is easily repaired. You can find them quite inexpensively at www.thegallery.us/hanger/

It's always wise to work with a level to make sure your pictures are hung correctly. You'll find these at any home improvement store as well. I have two: one small for small to medium sized pictures; one long for hanging large companion pictures. Just hold it against the wall and match up the bubbles on each side to find a level line.

Many stagers have fake food props. These can get expensive, so choose wisely if you plan to include them in your services.

Some are better quality than others. The jury is still out on just how "real" they should look. After all, you don't want any

buyer (or their children) to try to eat the food. Some fake food suppliers provide products to restaurants, who really DO want the food to look real.

But that might not be so great for a stager. Still in all, the idea is to make the dining table or the kitchen counter "come alive" with the suggestion that the kitchen is *perfect* for good cooks.

A search on the phrase "fake food" will bring up a bunch of sites to investigate.

If you're "going green", don't ruin it all by putting out a fake hot dog or other similar type of food. Purchase fake food that is considered healthy instead. Shop and compare as there is a wide range of prices and quality. Order just one and see what it looks like before buying more.

Naturally you don't want to put an actual computer or television in a staged home, but here is an example of a fake computer that is often seen in model homes or retail stores. You can purchase faux computers,
televisions and laptops and more at such sites as

PropsByID.Com or BoxProps.Com. Heck, there is even a faux washer and dryer set in plastic available. Prices vary by size of TV or other appliance. In some cases you must purchase more than one, so be careful before you buy. You can even have some items custom printed with your business contact information instead of the pictures they offer you. It's just another free and consistent way to advertise your services in the home (and keep your prop from being stolen at the same time).

Lo and behold, you can even use fake books. But before you go invest serious money into fake books, look in your local used book store or at the public library for books that you can buy on the cheap. Keep tabs on special library sales.

If you buy books that are all the wrong color for the home you're working in, cover them in white or off-white paper (temporarily), or turn the jackets to the wall and just let the pages show in the front. Kind of cool.

When you stop to think about it, there are solutions to every problem if you just open your mind and discover them.

P.S. Only buy hard bound books. They will withstand heavy moving better and will also look a whole lot better on shelves, whether their covers face out or inwards.

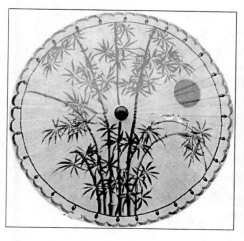

Another interesting and seldom used prop is the umbrella (parasol). Look for interesting patterns and designs to add an element of surprise to your decorating efforts. An added blessing is that these types of props are very light weight.
A nice selection can be found at www.jedicreations.com.

Air beds are great props that are light weight, easy to set up and easy to rent out. They are typically not high enough, but you can place cardboard boxes under them, cover with a large bedspread and no one will know it is not a real bed. Be sure and place a sign on the bed that says, "Please do not sit on bed. It is a prop." You can find air beds online or at your local camping stores. A queen size bed is a good size.

If you want to give yourself even more flexibility, consider getting an air sofa which can double as a bed. You can use it as a sofa in living rooms, family rooms, offices and dens. Or stick it in a bedroom as a bed. Type in "air bed" or "air sofa" and you'll find websites that sell these if you don't find them locally.

Folds out into a comfy bed!

Don't forget to spruce up that garden shed as well. It needs to be staged just like the home.

Stackable chairs are easy to purchase as props. Use them inside or outside. Try to choose a design that is light in weight but visually appealing.

As you can see, there is a very wide assortment of props you can either purchase to rent out or suggest that your clients purchase. These are from StarBamboo.Com. Incidentally clients can always include some or all of the props they provide with the sale of the house, either for profit or as an incentive for buyers to place an offer within a specified amount of time.

5 - Getting Paid!
How to Make Sure You Get Recognized for Excellence

Just A Small Handful of Students Who Are Growing Their Businesses in Staging and Redesign

While many people wonder if it's possible to become successful in home staging and redesign, there are many people who are realizing their dreams and building strong businesses. They studied. They asked questions. They got certified. They followed the training, both in design and marketing, and now they're realizing the rewards of their work. I thought you might like to meet a few of them.

Some of them enjoyed a quick journey to success. Others required more time to develop. Some faced extreme hardships along the way. Some had natural ability while others had to learn everything for the first time.

Some people start a business is absolutely no background whatsoever. Others have had other businesses in other types of industries. Some have been in business for a while but continue to educate themselves.

Where you come from has little bearing on your future success. Education comes first; action comes second; adaptation comes third.

129

As you can see from the examples shown on previous pages, home staging and redesign services are provided to homeowners within a wide range of socio-economic groups, with differing tastes and styles and with differing ages of home and furnishings. Some of the furnishings and homes are contemporary; many are not. Consultants are located all over the United States, Canada, Europe and Australia. When a project is handled correctly, and points brought up by agents and sellers are handled properly and efficiently, and you've established a clear record of what you began with and where the project ended up, this will help you increase your chances of being paid swiftly, but should you wind up in small claims court or superior court over compensation due to you, you'll have ample proof to prove you performed at the highest standards if you are well trained, organized and efficient.

There is no substitute for precise training in both interior design concepts and strong business strategies.

No matter what the economic climate while you're reading this, please understand that there will **always** be a dire need for home staging and redesign services. Most people do not know how to properly arrange the furnishings they own. Most people don't even want to learn how to do things properly. So they will rely on people like you to come along and do it for them.

Most people, in spite of the publicity about staging, still don't know what staging is all about. They predictably do not use staging techniques to sell their homes – not even the really obvious techniques. So, therefore, home stagers will always find there is a dire need for what they have to offer.

Your task is to ferret out the potential clients, educate them on the benefits, make your services available at a reasonable price, making sure every step of the way that you have protected your ability to get paid when all is said and done.

6 - Getting Paid!
Landing the Project
So You Can Make the Profit

Landing the project (also known as closing the sale) is of course vital to your success. Without the project you can't earn any money. So you get the client to agree to hire you, you get their signature on your agreement form, you go back to your office to collect formal contracts for signature and to send via certified mail and you begin to rejoice.

There is a phenomenon you should be aware of that can happen at this point. I've seen it happen when I was trying to purchase a home. And I've seen it happen when I've been

hired to manage a project.

Somehow, magically, you suddenly have competition!

Out of nowhere, someone wants to buy the home suddenly. Out of nowhere, another stager or re-designer shows up on the scene and wants to compete with you for the business.

Since this phenomenon happens with surprising regularity, you would do well to warn your client that it could happen and that such sudden interest from out of the blue is usually suspect and really not to be taken seriously.

Case in point: After sitting on the market vacant for half a year, we decided to make an offer on a condo for my partner. We weren't as happy with the neighborhood as we would have preferred, but other than that the property had nearly every requirement we wanted.

But because I already knew about the phenomenon of sudden competition, I told my partner that we should throw out a fleece to protect ourselves emotionally and mentally should competition arise. In a case like this, one really doesn't know if the sudden competition is real or fictional (all geared to get you to offer more), but we decided that if we had to negotiate against another real or imaginary buyer that we would immediately withdraw our offer.

And don't you just know it, as soon as our real estate agent placed our offer on the table, a magical competitive buyer appeared. I've taken extensive training in the stock market, and one of the concepts I've been taught is to decide on a profit target and a stop loss on every position BEFORE entering it. When you do that, and you abide by the rules you have set for yourself, you can then enter the trade without any emotion impacting your decisions. When the stock hits your profit target, you get out of the position and collect your profit. If the stock moves in the other direction, you're automatically taken out of the trade when your stop loss is hit. There are no emotions involved.

That, in essence, is what we did before we formulated our offer. We determined the maximum we were going to offer (and that's what we offered) and we said that if competition raised its ugly head, we were out. You see, I don't believe there was really any actual buyer competing for the house. I just don't believe in that type of coincidence being real. It always happens, but most of the time it's phony. I thought it was phony and when I think something is phony, I back out.

As it turns out, the decision to pass on the property was made about 6 months from the onslaught of sub prime foreclosures and massive home values dropping. Had my partner purchased that property, he would be upside-down right now. So he was saved from over bidding and getting caught by what's happened in the real estate market to date.

In case I haven't stated it to you before, my business philosophy is this: When in doubt, don't. I had restless feelings about this property even before we were told there was another offer on the table. So the fact there was supposedly competition in the works, I knew for sure it was a bad move for my partner to make. Fortunately I was right to terminate the offer.

As for magical competition in the form of another stager or re-designer, it's probably phony as well. But should you get some last minute professional trying to muscle their way into your project, don't be alarmed. If you've done your best to present yourself as a true professional worth every penny you ask for, your proposal should stand up against anyone.

Should an agent or homeowner try to renegotiate terms and pricing with you claiming to have just been contacted by a competitor, stand firm. Do NOT give into such tactics because 9 times out of 10 it's a rouse and there is no competition. More likely than not it's a last ditch attempt by the client to negotiate a lower price based on "buyer's remorse" or them second guessing their earlier decision.

Simply reassure them of your dedication to assisting them with the finest service, the most adept ideas and solutions and your willingness to jump through hoops on their behalf.

If you back down and offer to renegotiate you will lose their respect and you will set yourself up for more requests to lower your fees as you get further into the project. They will feel they have you imprisoned in their power trip and you will no longer be in control. I never let anyone negotiate me down. Never. In this manner I keep the flow of intimidation and power on my side of the fence, even in the face of what appears negative.

I've even had success when inferring to a prospect that he or she can't afford me or that we're not a "good fit". Just the act of denying someone your services somehow makes them want you all the more.

We're all that way really. We seem to always want what we feel we *can't* have and we don't want what we *can* have. It's true in male/female relationships. And it's true in business too.

It's natural for prospects and clients to want a better deal and to wonder if there is a better deal out there. Admit it. You've thought the same thing every time you're faced with a decision to buy or to sell.

If you've pre-warned your prospect or client that such offers might hit at the last moment and that they're not real, you'll really look professional to them because you predicted they would come. But you'll also go a long way in helping your client be suspicious of them since you already warned them ahead of time.

On top of that, you'll send a message loud and clear to your prospect or client that you are aware of such phony tactics and that you will not be fooled by them. Any way it goes down, you'll be a winner if you don't give into any pressure to lower your pricing or change the agreement you have made or will propose. I would rather lose a project or a sale and stand my ground than give in and feel down the road that somehow I got taken advantage of.

A serious client doesn't want to wait around for dickering and last minute competitors and such – not really. Once they have made a decision, they usually want to move forward quickly. So remember that and hang tough. You're more than likely the one who will be left standing when the "dust" settles.

Learning to Receive

Here's another good tidbit for you. One of the main reasons so many people are not successful at what they do is that they do not feel worthy to receive the rewards of their efforts. Somewhere along the way they began to feel they did not deserve success. Perhaps they were programmed by negative parents, friends or relatives or former bosses.

Whether you are actually worthy or not is not a factor. It's actually a lie you are telling yourself. You are the one who gives meaning to life and what you will accept or reject from it. I can assure you that God did not predetermine that one

 person should be successful and another person should not be successful. It just doesn't work that way.

You are the one who determines your worthiness to receive. You are the one who chooses to believe the lies. You are the one who determined your fate so far by how you chose to react to what life gave you in the past.

So if you say to yourself that you are not worthy, then you are not worthy. If you say you ARE worthy, then you are.

I can tell you this much. You will live out whatever belief you have of yourself. You are in charge of writing your own story. You will write the beginning, the middle and the ending. It is your story. You are the only writer.

I have 6 cats. I guarantee you than none of my cats feels unworthy of the food and shelter I provide to them. They expect me to feed them and keep them warm and happy. Humans are the only creatures in God's universe that have the ability to put limits on themselves. Animals don't engage in such destructive behavior or thought patterns.

If you are suffering from this malady, then change your story. It costs you nothing and you have everything to gain.

Write yourself a new story. Live **that** story.

Discard all negative statements about your worthiness from the past.
Write a whole new set of statements about how worthy you are of all of the blessings God has in store for you. Place these statements around your home and office. Read them often.

For every gift there must be a recipient. For every recipient there must be a giver. I trade in the FOREX (foreign exchange spot market). I trade the dollar against the other major currencies, such as the Euro, the Swiss franc, the British pound, the Australian dollar, the Canadian dollar and the Japanese yen.

In any given trade, one currency is up and the other currency in the pair is down. One up - one down. The idea is to guess successfully which currency will be up and which one will be down at any given time. Guesses are based on the currencies fundamentals, technical analysis and news from around the world. Guessing still is part of the equation and there is always risk. Guess wrong and you lose money; guess right and you gain profits.

There is, in that sense, a giver and a receiver. When you lose money, you're giving away your money. When you gain profit, you're receiving a monetary reward. There's no one out there defining who will gain and who will lose. No one says one investor is more worthy than another.

But of course if one isn't prepared properly and isn't trained properly, venturing into the currency market is completely foolish. But when one is trained and prepared, it can be financially rewarding.

Worthiness is not the issue. Training and preparation come first. Action comes second. There's a bit of luck too.

Ultimately, however, those that believe in their worthiness will be the only ones who will ultimately be successful because their story is based on the belief that they can and will succeed even if there are temporary setbacks.

This is how you must think.

If you do *not* write a story that makes you ready to receive success, then you are robbing those that want to give you that success. People stand ready and willing to do business with other people. Whether you are ready to receive their money or not, they are ready to give it. So if they don't give their money to you, they will give it to someone else. It's called competition. It's called business.

7 - Getting Paid!
Growing Your Profits Into Real Wealth

Turning Profits into Riches

Many people think that the way to get wealthy is to merely earn a lot of money. Well, they are only partially correct. It's true that you have to earn money, but the real secret to getting wealthy is not how much you earn – but how much you're able to keep.

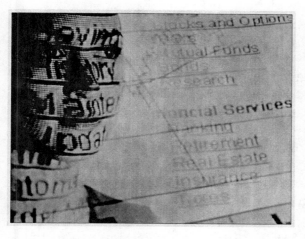

And even then, that's not the whole secret. You have to earn great sums of money, figure out how to keep as much as you can (lower taxes, lower expenses). Then you have to turn around and make your money work for you. As Harv Eker so brilliantly and simply states in his best selling book, "Secrets of the Millionaire Mind":

"Do you want some simple but extremely rare advice? Here it is: If you want to get rich, focus on making, keeping, and investing your money. If you want to be poor, focus on spending your money. You can read a thousand books and take a hundred courses on success, but it all boils down to that. Remember, what you focus on expands" (pg. 81).

If you have a successful business and you have too much work to do yourself, you typically think about hiring someone to help you. Unless that person is making you more money than you could make without them, that person is an additional expense, draining away your profits. If that person saves you more money than they cost you, that is one thing. But if that person is costing you more of your profits, you are losing money on the deal.

But what if you could take your profit and invest some of it passively so that the profit you have already earned is now making you even more profit? Would that not be pretty cool?

All too often (and I know this from personal experience) we are so tempted to spend our new found profits and enjoy some of the benefits of making more money, that we are not wise managers of our profits. I'm all for rewarding your self for your hard work – to a point. I have learned, however, after running rampant through some of my own early profits at record speed, that it would have been much more prudent to invest more and spend significantly less.

So I want you to avoid the pitfall I fell into. I have always been a spender, and much of my earlier years were spent living pay check to pay check, using my credit cards beyond good reason. I even made some foolish decisions regarding my home equity loan and mortgage, which later meant I had to pay out thousands of additional dollars to pay off my debt.

Debt is not good. Debt is not your friend. And the worst debt in the world is debt you incurred for benefits you enjoyed a very long time ago. To illustrate this, let me share a current situation unrelated to my business. Sometimes you can learn more from examples unrelated to business.

As I'm writing this section, we are in the midst of the Olympics. My son has dreamed since he was a young boy of making it to the Olympics. He was an outstanding triple jumper in high school and college, though he never made it to State or Nationals. He kept the dream alive, even though it was far fetched to me.

I learned when he was in high school to keep silent about his possibilities for success, because all too often he would surprise me and explode to the next level at the most surprising times when I thought the achievement was impossible.

So over the weekend he decided that he must travel to Beijing to witness and experience the Olympic atmosphere first hand. I advised him against going for a myriad of reasons, all practical. But his decision was based on emotions and the desire to let the experience be the catalyst to propel him over the next 4 years as he works to achieve his dream for the next Olympics.

He bought airline tickets, booked a hotel reservation, scouted the city for bus and subway transportation, noted the locations of the track venue and made a hasty trip to the Chinese Consulate for a last minute Visa. Then he took off for China, putting the entire cost on his credit card. I tried to change his mind using practical monetary wisdom but to no avail. Emotions won out.

I did, however, make sure he understood that once the euphoria of the trip and the excitement of being there wore off, he would find this one of the toughest debts to pay back. When you buy a home, you continuously live in and enjoy the home, so making the monthly payment isn't has hard. But when the enjoyment is essentially emotional and mental, paying back the money borrowed is very, very hard indeed because the enjoyment was so temporary.

So the best course of action is to avoid debt at all cost. Keep your expenses as low as possible. Plan your actions carefully and weigh the risks at all times. Set aside a specific percentage of your profits each month to invest so that you grow a separate income that has nothing to do with the ebb and flow of your business.

What is Your Net Worth?

Most people think that the measure of their worth is based on their income from a job or career or even their business. They base their thinking either on their gross income (what you earn before you pay taxes) or their net income (what you have left over once taxes and expenses are taken out).

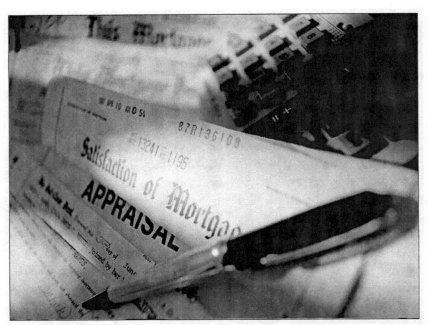

But your true worth is based on your *net worth*. Net worth is the figure you get when you add up the value of everything you own, such as your home, your vehicles, your possessions, your investments, your bank accounts and so forth. Once you add up the total value, then you subtract from that value the total amount of all your debts, such as your mortgage, your credit card balances, and any other debts you have. The figure that is left over (and hopefully you own a lot more than you owe) is your net worth.

Successful entrepreneurs recognize that the essential figure is based on a combination of assets less the combination of debts. This is why successful business people repeatedly and consistently add to their total assets. They don't look only at increasing their income from one source. They work all their assets and also work at lowering all debts.
Your work income is important, don't get me wrong. If you don't have money coming in routinely it's extremely difficult to save and get your savings working for you too. If you're spending all that you make, and even worse, borrowing money on a regular basis to sustain your life style or live beyond your means, you're going down a very dangerous road.

Ultimately you'll reach a point where you run out of the ability to borrow. And during economically stressful times, interest rates can run rampant. This is another reason why I hate to see people go into debt over business expenses and why we work hard to help students recoup their educational investment as soon as possible.

If you're still operating your business in the "red", meaning you haven't recouped the costs of learning the business and getting it all set up, then I hope you'll really delve into what I'm teaching in this book and really devote the time and energy necessary to work this system.

Your portfolio is a powerful extension of the essence of you, your talent, your education, your knowledge and your experience to date. It is a vital ingredient which you can use over and over again to propel you into a successful consulting business, whether your focus is on home staging or on redesign.

But never forget. Negotiate for the highest fees you can get without being unfair to your client. Make sure you get paid for all your time and effort. But don't rush out and spend all you make.

Feed that piggy bank or that savings account. Make your profits begin to work for you on a passive level while you continue to generate income on an active level. This is the best road to wealth and financial independence.

Managing Your Profits

This may surprise you but developing a habit of managing your money is more important than the amount you have to manage. This may come naturally to a few people, but most people need to learn the skills of money management and develop a habit. I will briefly relay some of my own habits.

I have a personal checking account and I have a business checking account. I have various investment accounts: Mutual Funds, Stocks and Options and a Forex Account. I have more than one life insurance policy. And I have several savings accounts in banks, treasuries and money market accounts. I also own some precious metals.

I have invested a lot of money in educating myself on a wide platform of financial strategies and I will always devote time and energy to further my education. Do you know how few people there are who are willing to buy a book and read in order to educate themselves? Congratulate yourself in being one who reads for improvement! You should never stop learning.

I wrote earlier that in my early business life I was a spender. I still enjoy my earnings, but I'm now much more focused on getting my income to work for me. Perhaps that's because

I'm older and wiser. I wish I had developed the habit of saving and investing earlier in life. But you can't look back. You have to decide today to improve your net worth and take one step at a time.

Try to live within your means and save at the same time. This is good money management and it will pay huge dividends to you in the future if you begin now and continue with your management plan all of your life. See a professional financial planner if you need to do so. But get educated and live wisely.

Set up several accounts: A long term savings account, an education account, a needs account, an emergency account and a giving account. Divide up your earnings into proportions that make sense to you. Put the percentage you have designated into each account on a monthly basis. Don't vary what you do unless you have suffered a massive emergency in your life. The majority of your income will go into your needs account, say 50% of your earnings. Split 30% between the education, long term and giving accounts, leaving 20% for unexpected expenses (emergencies).

In the end you will either control the profits you earn or your profits will control you. To be in control, you must manage properly. People who struggle only want to do what's easy. The result is that life is usually hard. People who are willing to do what's hard usually discover that life is easy (barring emergencies, of course).

Focus on Your Opportunities

Successful entrepreneurs focus on the opportunity ahead of them and not the obstacles. They don't wait until they feel they know everything. That is a waste of precious time. They recognize that knowing everything is impossible. They also recognize that they have the ability to make adjustments as they go along.

They spend diligent effort and time to learn what they can learn in as short a time frame as possible. Then they take action. As they begin and start to grow their business, they take the necessary corrective actions along the way. Unsuccessful people focus on their fears and tell themselves they need to know more before they can start. This is just a delaying tactic. Don't fall for it.

Go ahead. Start. Nothing happens without action. Don't wait for the "perfect time". There is opportunity everywhere no matter what type of economy exists at the moment.

But opportunity waits for no one. You've got to take action – and the sooner the better.

Focus on Promotion

Successful entrepreneurs are willing to promote their business – which essentially means promoting themselves. As consultants we can really only promote our way of thinking and our way of acting. It boils down to our knowledge and talent.

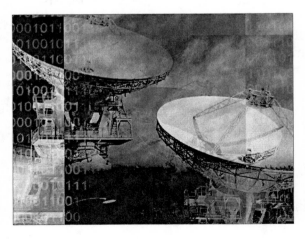

I've had a few people get really angry at me after reading some of my earlier books because I whole heartedly promoted my knowledge and expertise and products that I had created or pulled together from other sources which I believed would help them become successful and take much of the time, effort and pain out the process of launching and recouping their investment.

The people who persecuted me were not taking issue with my training strategies and concepts. They got angry because I told them about products that would help them succeed. It always astonished me, because I was not only trying to help them succeed rapidly, I was demonstrating how you can weave other products and services into what you offer your clients – by what you say or by what you write on a website or in a newsletter or some other material you might want to create.

But the people who got angry at me for this (and occasionally still do) are arguably people who think negatively about selling and promotion. By the way, I'm certainly not alone in the strategy I have used and I'm certainly not the only author to reap a backlash from negative thinkers.

My experience is the same as other authors. Most people are thrilled and appreciate getting notice about other courses or products available for them to consider. But there are a small percentage of people who resent any promotion regardless of how it might benefit them.

Are you someone who resents promotions? If you are, you probably should take note of that characteristic about yourself. I'm serious. Resenting promotion is one of the greatest obstacles to success. People who resent the selling and promotion of other people are almost always broke or quite possibly jealous.

Look at it this way. If you aren't willing to let people know that your business exists and how you can benefit them, how will you ever make any success of it? Think about your life as someone's employee. If you never made any attempts to promote your virtues to your boss, someone else probably came along and bypassed you on the corporate ladder who was willing to promote their assets.

I'm not saying that every sales or promotional attempt that comes to you from another business is presented appropriately or in a timely manner or that you have never experienced the telemarketer who refuses to take "no" for an answer. That would irritate anyone. But many times people over react to past experiences that they did not appreciate and push that negativity off on all future offers regardless of how they are presented or how they might be beneficial.

Perhaps you've tried to promote yourself in the past and were rejected and the whole experience was so distasteful to you that you now react negatively toward promoting yourself further. If so, you need to realize that the past experiences you have had (whether good, bad or neutral) have no bearing on the future.

Or perhaps you were taught in your youth that you should never "blow your own horn" — that such behavior is bragging and bad manners. If so, you need to realize that when it comes to business and money, if you don't promote your virtues boldly, no one else will do it for you and you will soon be out of business.

Successful entrepreneurs will tell anyone about their business.
Successful entrepreneurs will promote their business aggressively.
Successful entrepreneurs will try to do business with anyone and everyone.
Successful entrepreneurs will never stop promoting their virtues, their services and their products. Never.

That's what this book is all about. Giving you the tools to promote your business with power, sensibility, tenacity and consistency.

Overcome Promotional Resistance

I want you to know that if you suffer from resistance to promotional tactics (whether promotions are directed your way or whether you're advancing your own promotions) you can overcome these hang-ups. I did. I can remember when I first started in a sales position as a corporate art consultant. I had owned a graphic design business and I had failed at a wicker/rattan retail business. I just was terrified to promote my business and products to other people.

By forcing myself to do it any way, even when I initially failed, I eventually overcame my fears and hesitations. It took time and it took conscious effort. But I did it. So can you.

One of the concepts that helped me early on was recognizing that if I REALLY believed in my own value, if I REALLY believed in the benefits of my service and products, then I was doing my prospects an immense disservice by not sharing information about how I could help them.

I began to view it as rudeness on my part to withhold such information. When I was able to restructure my thinking and my feelings, my actions changed to match my new feelings about my value and the value of what I was promoting.

Will people still reject what I am offering to them? Yes they will. That's part of business. But when you change how you think and feel about yourself and your services, your level of enthusiasm and genuineness will go up – way up. And people will evaluate you in a totally different manner. Refusals will diminish. You'll just have to trust me on that issue.

Enthusiasm is contagious. Genuinely presented benefits will be attractive to others. All things being equal, you're bound to increase your success. With every step forward, your confidence will rise. People hire confident people.

Hone your presentation skills as you go. Trust yourself. You will get better and better and better. Pretty soon you will look back and wonder what the big deal was and won't be able to remember why you were afraid in the first place. Instead of resenting others for promoting their products and services to you, study what they are saying to you and doing. Be appreciative of them. You can learn a lot from watching

others. Do what you see them doing, in your own style. Develop a habit of studying the marketing techniques of others, regardless of their industry group. Be grateful, not resentful.

When you do that you will move a long way forward with your own business, not just in the short term, but in the long term as well.

My Final Challenge to You

We've covered a lot of ground together. I've emphasized many important tactics and strategies, goals and options. Now there's just one more point I want to make. Naturally when you go into business, you want to be successful. Success is usually defined by how much profit you make. I've talked about the importance of making a profit, but also the greater importance of *keeping* the profit. I've talked about maximizing profit and minimizing expenses. I've discussed net income and the greater importance of net worth. I've talked about fear and resistance to the need for constant promotion.

Now I want to finish up by saying this. Business is quite a bit like athletics. You could certainly look upon it as a game. It will be a game you will either win or lose – and you may be up one day and down the next day.

Your competition may come from other people or it may come from your own past performance and a desire to hit a higher high. Today you may have decided that you have failed. Or perhaps you're brand new and haven't established a track record yet or you're an old hand and just looking for an edge.

There are many types of entrepreneurs. There are those who will care only about winning – about being the best – about earning the most – about getting all the publicity and notoriety. For them, coming in second doesn't count. They want "olympic gold" and nothing short of gold will satisfy them.

While this may sound contradictory at first, my challenge to you is simply to be good. And to do good for others. We only travel this way once and the path is a short path. Be a good person. Do good for others. Everything else will take care of itself eventually.

Yes, money is important. You can accomplish a lot of things with money. But attaining vast sums of money is not going to bring you happiness. At first you'll have the thrill of the success. But the longer the success is sustained, the more it will turn to the mundane and monotonous.

But when you lend a hand to someone else, there's no feeling like it in the world. And no matter how many times you do good for someone else, especially in the face of hardship or turmoil in your own life, the more rewarded you will feel.

Be good. Do good. And you will be happy regardless of the balance in your bank account.

8 - Getting Paid!
Some Questions and Answers

Questions and Answers

QUESTION

Hello Barb, I loved your course & have done a few staging jobs. Thanks for providing such good material.

I need some expert biz. advice though- I'm finding it's a headache to house furniture & accessories. How would you stage vacant properties and accessorize without maintaining so much inventory? How can I get that monkey off my back? How can I have the client provide those things?

ANSWER

The easiest answer I can give you is to set your rules of what you will and won't do and abide by them no matter what. That's the beauty of being self employed. You don't have to do anything you don't want to do.

So you just say, "Your home needs furniture and accessories to heighten its assets and reach out to the emotions of prospective buyers. You'll dramatically increase your opportunities to sell quickly and at the highest profit if the house is relatively furnished. You'll shoot yourself in the foot financially if you leave it empty. My company does not furnish what you need, but I'll be more than happy to professionally arrange and place everything that is brought into the house for me to use. When can you make arrangements to rent or borrow enough furnishings to make the house feel like a home?"

Then be prepared to walk away if they choose not to bring anything in for you to work with. Simple. ·The problem with most people is they want the job so much they compromise themselves and get in above their tolerance for risk (purchase and warehousing of props). That's when their business get into jeopardy.

> So set your rules. Draw the line. Don't cross over it for anyone for any reason. And focus instead on finding the type of client YOU want to have - your ideal client - and forget the rest.

Rule #1 - I never accept a verbal staging project.

Rule #2 – I never travel more than 45 minutes each way to a project.

Rule #3 – I never accept a project without a budget.

Rule #4 – I never accept a project from a client I dislike.

This isn't a complete list of my personal rules, but I think you get the point, right?

If you set rules, you'll remove a lot of the emotion from the situation and you'll be making choices and accepting projects with your head and not your heart. You'll automatically become more discriminating about what you will accept as a good project and you'll find it a whole lot easier to walk away from the ones that are not ideal for you.

No one can set these rules for your business except you. Your risk tolerance and the level of service you choose to provide can only be determined by you. There will be some stagers who have no problem with acquiring and renting out their own props. There will be others that couldn't do that even if they wanted.

So just make the best decisions for you that you're capable of making and then worry not about your decisions.

QUESTION

I regularly view other stager's sites just because you have to know what the competition is doing. Quite a few of the room views have me yawning instead of having me at Hello. I like a room to convey a warm welcoming atmosphere but with a little sizzle too. Something unusual or memorable that will have people talking about the space long after they leave. Barb asked in another section that we post our most unusual accessory and none of us have.

So Barb, do you have some current favorites? What constitutes to too much versus too little for pizzazz in a room provided we avoid re-cluttering the space and the sparkle plenty syndrome?

ANSWER

This is a very interesting point you bring up and the answer is not easy, obviously. Delving into the area of "sizzle" in staging really boils down to a particular stager's own creativity, good taste, flair for drama and just good decorating talent. The notion that staging is not decorating, that it's just real estate, is silly when judged from this criteria. But that's what many people are being taught, so what emerges will tend to be bland and boring and expected, or done badly, because they were not taught the design concepts they should know and implement.

Then there's the difficulty of achieving some kind of real design essence yet keeping the home neutral enough to be more accepting to more buyers. And there's the point of knowing when you've done enough or even if the budget will allow you to do enough (more likely scenario of the two these days).

So how do you get pizzazz without overdoing it? The answer lies in the accessories.

Few people realize it but personality and individuality, flair, drama and instant appeal are mainly expressed through accessories, not furniture, not drapes, not carpets or floors. But few people put good money and flair into their choice of accessories, buying mostly small, cheap stuff. That's why when you go into most homes, the art (if there is any) is small or medium in size. Plants are also small as are all the other accessories. It's as if people are afraid to invest in anything large or bold or artistic. I can't believe it's strictly an economic thing. I really think they just don't know what they're doing so they think "having something" is better than not having anything, so they buy a bunch of small stuff so they have "plenty of stuff", but it's practically worthless stuff and they scatter it all around to "fill up the space" and then it all looks cluttered and overly busy and they're disappointed. So they go out and buy more small stuff and scatter it around some more, making the problem twice as bad as it was before.

Or they go to the other extreme, and buy nothing, and then they have nothing to express their personality or uniqueness. The house is bare and boring, but rather than put some money into quality accessories of substance, they go put bold colors all over the walls thinking that will liven things up. Well, it not only livens things up, it overpowers the rooms and they have accomplished nothing of real value and usually the home now feels ghastly because the colors are too overwhelming and exhausting.

Small accessories are filler and must be combined with medium and large accessories to work at all. So there has to be groupings. But that leads to clutter.

So the answer for stagers is looking to incorporate a few very large accessories: huge painting, huge mirror, indoor trees, large pottery, large floral arrangements. And the more artistic the better. But since the average stager is on a limited budget and storage is a problem, they tend to purchase small "props", so the problem continues.

It costs serious money, as stagers will have to inventory these types of accessories, as the homeowners aren't going to have them and renting them may be equally difficult. So stagers need to look for very large accessories, of a neutral palette, that have class and drama and artistic elements: great composition in the art - beautiful and never bizarre - dramatic rather than traditional - unique rather than run-of-the-mill - contemporary rather than ultra ornate. You're not going to find the right types of accessories shopping at thrift shops, Walmart, Target, Kmart, garage sales and the like. Because they are "small stuff" specialists - run-of-the-mill sellers - non-artistic peddlers of cheap, see-everywhere stuff. While the prices are good, what you find is "ordinary".

And if stuck with ordinary accessories, stagers need to have a flair for arrangement design, working more with asymmetrical design rather than symmetrical (unless in a really traditional environment).

You can't accomplish this without strong design skills or natural talent and a heap of "daring" thrown into the mix.

If large or artful accessories are simply out of the question, then perhaps daring to do something neutral (yet bold) on an accent wall will do the trick. Pull out your own unique creativity and artistic talent and go for it. But only if you're good. One also has to note the architecture of the home and draw emphasis to unique features of the "shell". Sometimes attention gets thrown too much to other aspects of staging, forgetting that there were some really obvious places architecturally that could have been enriched with high drama with just some well placed paint or wallpaper.

If you can't do that, be happy with providing an "ordinary" staged home, which is going to be better than a pre-staged home, even if it doesn't have anyone especially saying "HELLO" or "WOW". That's ideal, of course, but can't always be achieved, especially if budgets are extremely limited or don't exist.

QUESTION

I've read most of your books and I was going to take the tests for certification this morning but . . . I'm hesitating and trying to discern the value.

ANSWER

The real value is in how you use your certification and directory listing to establish credibility for you and your knowledge and talents. While certification does not guarantee success in and by itself, it sure does help, especially in a highly competitive area. So one should not look solely on what a directory listing will generate for your business as much as being able to promote your business as being included and recognized as legitimate and well grounded. Our certification process is tougher to get by design, because we believe candidates who achieve it should first prove they have the knowledge and ability to perform.

When one can say to a potential client that they had to pass an exam and submit a portfolio to be reviewed before attaining their designation, it is very powerful and persuasive. Look on these as "investments" in credibility and competitive power, as well as a means to be found and contacted. Certification also builds personal confidence.

So each person has to decide the value - and most times the real bona fide value in what you do is how you "market" those achievements and listings and how you talk about them in your daily business.

QUESTION

Have any of you gals taken on a project and then wished you hadn't because your name would be associated with it? I agreed to clean and partially stage a large house for a foreign doctor and his wife. Their realtor is a friend and cleaning client that gets me work with her buyers and sellers whenever she can.

I knew going in that whatever staging I did, the negatives in this big house would outweigh the positives. The house has a cold feeling to it because of having very little carpet, no window treatments. The sellers downsized and left some furniture to work with, which helped a bit, but nothing could change a bright red garden tub, red and white tiles, gold fixtures and pink marble countertops and walls in the master bath. The big great room walls were painted with three different tropical colors. There are additional colors in the dining room and entry. The owners were willing to repaint the extra bedrooms, mainly because the walls were dirty. But that was it with putting any money into updates. We did make some good in some of the rooms, but others couldn't be staged very well. They tried to sell before with no luck and it looks like they won't have much luck this time either. It's been on the market now since last summer. If I had a place to store all the things we put in the house, I would bring them back home and take my cards out.

So, my question is should you accept a project knowing that your name will be on it to get experience or pass it up knowing that it won't be a really good example of your talent as a stager?

ANSWER

This sounds like a horror story.

To answer your question I have the following comments.

First, your reputation and self image is all you really have that, once damaged, are very difficult to get back. So to me (having been in a couple of similar situations in the past), my reputation and my good feelings after the project work is finished are far more important to me than the money. If you know going in that the situation will still be hopeless afterwards, you will feel embarrassed to have anyone know you were connected with it, even if you could explain the situation.

It's just not worth feeling embarrassed and once your reputation is damaged, you can't get it repaired. So it's better to pass the project up.

The only difficulty in this situation is that you're connected with a friend that gets you work from time to time.

I would definitely tell the friend and anyone else you can that you want NO CREDIT for this project unless the owners give you the means to correct the problems.

If a project is bad and you are stifled from doing what needs to be done, then what kind of experience have you gotten anyway? None. You **can't** use the before and after pictures to promote your talent. So apart from some temporary

161

money, you've gained nothing and have everything to lose on the backend regarding your reputation.

These are choices that every stager must make. This manual has dealt with the subject of choosing projects based on whether there is sufficient profit in the deal to justify the effort and whether you feel there will be problems in getting paid.

But you also have to choose projects based on whether you can really make the kind of change that will lead to selling the house – because that is the end goal of all parties concerned, from the sellers to the agent to you. If you will be unable to achieve the end goal (whether it be the stubbornness of the owners or for lack of funds or whatever the case may be), then the whole project will be a waste of your time and talent and certainly apt to do damage to your reputation and your personal integrity as well.

To do otherwise is to say, in reality, that the money was worth more to you than the end goal and is not in the best interest of your client, much less you. I have a motto that says that if something is worth doing, it's worth doing WELL. No amount of profit is worth it to me if I cannot hold my head up afterwards and feel proud of the work I did.

So when you put it into this frame of reference, it is much better to say to the owners, "Look if you're going to pay for professional staging, then you owe it to yourself to do it right. With the tiny budget you're prepared to spend and the restraints you're placing on me, I cannot in good conscience accept this project. I would be doing you a disservice and I would be operating at a level beneath my personal standards for my business. I'm afraid under these circumstances I will not be able to accept the project. I wish you all the best."

Then walk away.

9 - Getting Paid!
How to Make Sure You Survive Hard Economic Times

Twelve Tips for Success During Economic Draw Downs

No one can deny that during economic turbulence businesses struggle to grow and many struggle to maintain their positions in the marketplace. Many others fail and go out of business. As clients pull back in their spending, we all feel the pinch in one way or another.

So let's discuss here some tips that will help you should you face a difficult period in your business, whether now or down the road.

- *Immerse yourself in excellence*, surrounding your self solely with people who have great attitudes and who have strong work ethics. I'm not talking about average people; I'm talking about above average people. People will influence your feelings, your attitude, your decisions, your actions. You don't want to be dragged down by negative, lazy people – whether they are your clients, vendors or family and friends.
- *Discover more creativity within yourself* – When you are marketing a product or service that other people are also marketing, the only thing that differentiates you from your competition is **you**. No one can compare with you, an individual. You have your own

unique set of talents, skills, creativity, knowledge, experience, dedication, commitment and fortitude. So what else can you bring to your business that you aren't currently offering and how can you highlight that uniqueness to set your business apart and above all others? Know your strengths and enhance them in your marketing messages. Know your weaknesses and work on them to eliminate them or at least to downplay them.

- *How can you improve your client services*? Everyone wants great customer service when they choose to do business. But not every company has great service. Some have terrible service. So how can you improve on your method of operation that will be noticeable to your prospects and clients? This even includes your vendors and sub-contractors.

- *When was the last time you reviewed your pricing guidelines*? When economic times change, and particularly during times of inflation or recession, companies typically change their prices. You've got to remain solvent and you've got to supply the financial needs of running your business at a profit. The dilemma everyone faces is whether to raise prices, whether to keep them level or whether to lower prices (counting on more volume to make up the difference). No one can advise you on what's best for your business, but don't be afraid to charge more. Whatever your prices are, stand by them. Make sure all policies are in writing and draw up the appropriate contracts to protect your interests.

- *Increase your referral generating systems*. One of the reasons for developing strong relationships with contacts and clients is so that you can contact them for referrals. Look for ways to offer some incentives to trigger more referrals coming your way. Word of mouth and personal references are vital to your on-going success. But you need to advertise and promote as well because nowadays it takes more than referrals to sustain a business.

- *Work at becoming an expert*. Specialization has never been more important than now. Don't think people automatically know what our industry does. They could have a misguided perception. Spend time and energy educating people in your area.
- *Host a seminar, fund raiser or other social event*. Social events are great places to stand out, especially when you are the lead speaker. There's just something in everyone that causes them to want to hook up with a speaker for goods and services. But you've got to be well prepared and have strong speaking skills or it can work against you.
- *Look for ways to form Strategic Partnerships*. It's tough to go it all alone. There are many related businesses that will be happy to "partner" with you for the good of everyone. Generate joint advertising campaigns. Contact other companies that are related but not competitors. Look for new ways your service and products can benefit people with a different value system currently. When times are tough, priorities change for the consumers on the lower end of the economic scale, but there are opportunities still.
- *Look for ways to up sell and back sell former clients*. People who have already done business with you in the past are more likely to do business with you in the present and future if you only take the time to be in some kind of rhythmic contact with them. Vary your approach. But remind them that you can still help them more with new ideas and creativity.
- *Never panic or give up*. Just as there are draw downs in the stock market, there will be draw downs in your business. That's the nature of being in business. During the hard times, you learn to tighten up your "ship" by checking your method of operating, your expenses, your income and opportunities. We always emerge from economic down turns and when we do, if you have worked hard to make your business better during the rough times, you will emerge an even stronger, more profitable company when the

economic climate is better. So don't give up. As people stay home more, their living space becomes even more important to them than before. It becomes more necessary for them to transform the home into a comfortable refuge. Redesign services are tailor made for times like these.

- *Step Up Your Networking Efforts.* Networking means more than just joining an organization or trade group or participating in a charity. You've got to get involved: get on a committee, make a name for yourself, be up in front, ask often how you can help. Set a goal to meet more people. Network wherever you go.
- *Improve your customer service and overall value.* People will search harder and do more comparison shopping. Beef up your value and make it easy for people to compare.

Reasons to Advertise in a Tough Economy or a Good One

Advertising is always a necessary part of building any business, but when times are tough many businesses cut back or stop their advertising altogether. Of course, you've got to make decisions about this based on many factors. You've got to factor in the expense of advertising against your expectations of what it will generate when people are curtailing their spending. This is not easy.

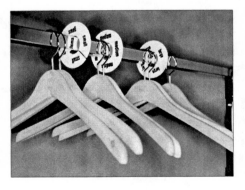

Some areas are always worse hit than others. But studies have shown that even in dire circumstances nearly half (41%) of consumers say a poor economy will not affect their spending habits. So that's quite assuring – and your job is to reach the 41% that will keep on spending.

So you're really faced with two choices:

- You can pull in your checkbook, ration out your resources, cut expenses where ever possible, batten down the hatches, lower your anchor, tie off the rudder and ride out the "storm".
- Or you can position yourself at the helm, keep your sails up, head straight into the wind, pull up your anchor and plow through the waves with a strong marketing and advertising plan.

Many successful business owners and executives think that advertising during a down economy is very important and here is their reasoning:

- *There will always be buyers.* It is extremely rare that an entire industry would completely fail, even those that are weaker to begin with. Even though there is a heavy toll as of this writing in the real estate market, the fact of the matter is that the vast majority of homeowners are paying their mortgages on time and in no fear of foreclosure. Less than 2% are in jeopardy or have already fallen prey to the foreclosure axe.
- *During down cycles, it's a media buyer's market.* I'm not saying you should jump into media advertising (print, TV, radio, online) but it is a time when media sellers will work more closely with you and offer you extra incentives that can have a nice impact on your budget.
- *Since buyers are not looking to spend, they need a reason to buy.* So it is up to businesses to provide those reasons. Your advertising should explain why your service is deserving of attention, why it's needed and beneficial, and why now is the time to act.
- *You'll get their attention easier.* When fewer businesses are advertising, it's easier to get your

message through. Have you noticed that you're getting less junk mail these days? When times are tough, it's easier to get your message to your target market and have it be remembered.

- *Gaining new customers can cost you less.* With better rates and fewer competitors vying for the consumer's attention, this is the time to take advantage of the advertising opportunities out there. This is a time to gain market share over your competitors if you can afford to do so.

Coping With Changing Times

Many people resist change. I can understand that, but change is inevitable in life – and especially in business. You've got to be able to adapt and change as the marketplace dictates. But don't fear. Change can often be so good it propels your business to new heights and new profits.

Change really *does* do a company good if you're open to it! You can go from stale and predictable to dynamic and cutting-edge, practically overnight in some cases.

Change does not have to be geographic, though that can energize you and any staff you have as well. Positive change can be **something as simple as changing your customary *approach* to a typical problem** or situation. It can be extremely subtle or it can be a major change.

So ask yourself this question: Is there something I've been doing for a long time because "that's the way I've always done it" even though I haven't been getting a good result from it for ages? Remember that nothing is written in stone. Consider letting go of what you've always done or feel comfortable doing, and change it up to a NEW idea or solution that has a better chance of providing a better result in the ever changing business environment.

Do you worry that if you take time to stop for lunch, you'll be your competitor's lunch? I used to feel that way. Perhaps a positive change can be something as simple as making a few alterations to your personal life. **You'd be amazed how much MORE productive you could be if you took** some time off to have some fun! Take a break and go for a walk in the park, for instance. Walking has always been a source of real idea creation for me – sort of like a moving think tank. My partner and I try to walk together at the park nearly every day. We get an enormous amount of discussions accomplished – often the discussions center around business and often they center around family and spiritual matters – all productive.

But BEFORE you dig out your old walking shoes or start throwing out the old ways and bringing in the new ideas, remember that change -- even small change -- can be nerve racking, *unless* you've prepared yourself in advance for it. Successfully managing change is all about your attitude and expectations and ability to roll with the punches.

Here are THREE things to consider before you take any change plunge:

1. What will it cost NOT to keep the status quo – or what will it cost to keep things the way they are?

I'll bet that whenever you consider the possibility of making a change, the first thing you think about is what it's going to cost you to do it. And if you're like me, that potential extra cost might be a deal-breaker.

So I'd like to encourage you to turn that around in your thinking: How much money will I LOSE by sticking with the same ol', same ol' processes, even though they're no longer really working for me?

2. What's the WORST that can happen vs. what's the BEST that can happen?

Many people let fear of the unknown stop them from making changes. After all, nobody can really say for SURE that a particular change will be as successful as you think it'll be -- and it *could* be a downright failure.

So before you make your change, ask yourself these questions: What's the *worst* thing that can happen if the change fails to produce the results I want? Is the failure a short term one or a long term one?

Be realistic in your answer and as objective as possible. Even if things *do* go awry a bit in the beginning, the net benefit might STILL outweigh the short-term draw down, and often the glitches can usually be a lot more easily managed or corrected than you might think leading to a long term trend upward.

3. Who will you count on for help, encouragement and support?

If you're prone to feeling worried or stressed out by change, then you'll *definitely* want people you trust to "talk you down" when you're feeling anxious about what's happening to your business.

Knowing you've got a solid safety net beneath you can make it MUCH easier to commit to implementing your changes. This is another reason why I wrote in the very beginning about the importance of surrounding yourself with positive, encouraging people and reducing from your life those who are negative and critical.

Change can often turn a stagnant, mediocre business into a more dynamic (and profitable) one, but it can also be a time of uncertainty and expense. By spending a bit of time BEFORE you make any change preparing yourself *mentally and emotionally* for that period of instability, you'll successfully manage any problems that arise and enjoy the rewards of an invigorated business!

4. How will you handle certain risks?

Even in the best of economic times, I advise you to keep the rental agreement for the large furniture (at least) between the home owner and the rental agency – not you. Many clients will perform well if you set it up for them to pay you. But it's the ones that don't that concern me. You don't need to take on that risk.

All you have to do is insist that the rent be paid by the homeowner directly to the rental company. They are set up to handle such arrangements, with the proper insurance and transportation processes. You are not. You may still be involved in picking out what is to be rented, making arrangements for delivery and pick up, but tell the homeowner that all costs associated with renting furniture is between the owner and the rental company. If you want to furnish accessories for rent, that's separate as well.

Publicity Still Pays Off

What makes publicity so outstanding is that it is free to you and your message will get out to thousands, even millions, of people. You can't buy advertising at that magnitude. And when you and your business are featured by the media, it acts like a 3rd party endorsement. People always respond strongly to what the media says about you whereas they might not react at all about what you say about you.

But getting publicity is downright difficult. Producers of TV shows and editors of magazines and newspapers are constantly inundated with press releases, press kits, emails, phone calls and faxes. They are literally swamped and don't have the time nor the energy to sift through everything that comes across their desk to weed out the good from the bad, the relevant from the irrelevant.

So you've got to figure out how you can bypass the pile on top of their desk.

You not only want to bypass the pile, you want to be remembered. You want to get "top of the mind status" with media people. And the only (or best) way to get into the top of their minds is by meeting them face to face.

I don't care what business a person has, the best way to build it is through relationships. I'm sure you already know this. So right about now you're probably asking yourself: "How do I get face to face with media people."

If you're in a large metropolitan area, there probably is a Press Club. Join it. Attend faithfully. You will meet media people there and have a chance to build relationships with them.

Attend trade shows. Media people usually come to industry trade shows and they are already interested in the topic of the show.

Develop a strong press kit with a strong headline as a hook. What is it about you or your service or product that is different from everyone else? Learn how to differentiate yourself from your immediate competition. Focus on how you will be a benefit to listeners or readers.

As you meet the media, you'll want to give them information about you and your business. Make your press kit as professional as you can because, remember, you'll always have a ton of other people competing for that same media person's attention. Be persistent. Be consistent.

Master the Art of Talking Points

Whenever possible, get rid of formal speeches and canned pitches. Talk informally. You will find your audience or prospect will be able to relate to you far easier when your conversation is "off the cuff". But to be sharp in an informal manner, you need talking points.

172

Talking points allow you to make major points quickly and effectively. And in a world where you will only have 10 seconds (if that) to get your message out, you need to do so quickly and effectively.

The idea is to get your idea out quickly and worry about the details later. Let your more important thought penetrate first. As time permits, you can always support the point later. People find it easier to remember your points when delivered in short, concise statements.

EXAMPLES:

- I jazz up your home to sell quickly.
- I work to get multiple buyers competing to purchase.
- I know when enough is enough.
- I'm every seller's best friend and advisor.
- There's no home I can't stage to sell better.
- I'll be done before you know it.

Talking points help your audience or prospect remember what you said. Stories are very powerful and well remembered as well. But talking points are short and sweet and the more they are filled with value, the better they are.

STAGERS HELP DREAMS COME TRUE

A few descriptive words will trump a long winded dissertation every time. So work at honing down your comments. Home staging and interior redesign are very closely related concepts, but home staging is a paired down, honed down concept. Interior redesign is a fully developed concept. And you have to look at your speech the same way. Once you've identified your central message, get it out there front and center. Incorporate short powerful sound bites into your marketing materials, on your website, in your statements.

Black Belt Marketing Strategies

Let's say economic challenges continue (most likely) or even get worse (very likely). How does a dedicated consultant

sustain their new or growing business and even grow it further? What are some of the current strategies for building on the success one already has? Here are some basic and stable methods that work very effectively and are crucial to your success.

Secret #1: Watch who you hang around with

A stager shared an apartment with her partner, a very good friend. They collaborated on several projects. But eventually the partnership began bit by bit to sour as conflicts in direction, personal goals and commitment took their toll.

While I encouraged her to exit the partnership, in part to gain peace of mind and in part to preserve what remained of the friendship, she was naturally reluctant. She hoped things would improve. But after suffering more failed promises and lack of commitment from her partner, the decision was inevitable.

Move out or get destroyed. So on the evening of the close of the Olympic games in Beijing, she packed up her belongings and exited the toxic environment.

Why was this decision critical?
Toxic relationships deplete your energy. They depress your spirit. They are like acid to your confidence and well being. And though you try your best to control and diffuse their power, it is usually a losing battle because you are powerless to affect the actions of other people. You can only control your own actions. I must say that partnerships are difficult, even in the best of situations. But when things go awry, they rarely improve to where they were before.

The time had come for the stager to "cut her losses" and move on. With help and support from her family, who love her unconditionally, she did just that. Following the abrupt change in her living situation, she soon doubted the wisdom of her decision, but time healed that and she now looks back on that day as a pivotal moment in her career. Lo and behold, the partnership has improved and they continue to be friends.

You must strive to rid yourself of toxic relationships that are eating away at your success and future happiness. You must recognize them for what they are and take the necessary steps to separate yourself, as much as possible, from negative influences in your life. Your business depends on it.

Your business and personal relationships will determine the level of success you will attain. So don't waste your time connecting with or collaborating with people and other businesses that are negative, unsupportive and unreliable. Look for people you can trust. Build relationships with people of integrity. Get your training and on-going support from a true master in the industry who has sustained the ups and downs of decades in the business. Emulate what you see them doing. Base your advertising, your promotions and your business practices the methods in keeping with the highest standards. Be smart. Be wise. Be honorable.

A friend's former roommate engaged in extremely destructive behavior that will follow the roommate for decades to come. The Bible says that if you are not trustworthy in small things, you will not be trustworthy in big things. When you see that someone close to you is unreliable, untrustworthy, vicious in their words, deceptive, self serving or a host of other dishonorable behavioral acts, move on quickly and don't look back.

It is easy at moments like this to feel you have wasted precious time you will never get back. In some industries, time is of the essence. So losing 3 years of one's professional life is bound to create regret.

But I will tell you the same thing I told her. Never look back with regret. No matter what has happened in the past, it has little bearing on what will or can happen in the future (unless you let it – be it positive or negative). You have been molded by the experiences you have encountered, the people you have met, the successes and failures you have experienced. You are who you are today because of where you've been in the past.

One can only make the best decision today one is capable of making. Hindsight is always nice, but we don't ever have the advantage of hindsight. Even if we did, many of us wouldn't make a different decision anyway. So be proud and determine to make the best decisions today that you are capable of making today given the information you have at your disposal today. That's all any of us can do.

Don't ever look back with regret. Instead use the painful or unproductive experiences of your past to propel you further. If someone has doubted your talents, use that doubt to motivate you at a deeper level in the future.

If you watched the men's 4x100 swimming relays at the Olympics, you saw Michael Phelps and teammates pull off a stunning upset against the French team. In part it was because one of the French swimmers had boasted earlier that they had come to "squash" the USA team.

That foolish statement by the French athlete was the additional fuel the USA team needed to turn in a truly amazing performance, take the Gold medal away from the French and break the world record in the process.

What business Gold Medal will you strive to earn next? What business record will you break soon? What motivation will you use to accomplish your next dream?

Secret #2: Consistency is the key for long-term success

Every Monday through Friday I'm busy at work doing whatever I feel I need to do that day to progress my business.

I rarely take time off and when I do I use the time for creativity and relaxation.

The point is I'm consistent. I'm persistent. I may not have strong will power when it comes to losing weight. OK, I admit it. But it's a very different story when it comes to my business.

My goals are not monumental. I'm not looking to be the Donald Trump in this industry. My goals challenge me and are reasonable. But like any other goals anyone would have, my goals require a level of consistent effort on my part.

Secret #3: Ups and downs are part of the process

The road to success does not move in a straight line. Just look at the stock market and the world currencies that are continuously fluctuating up and down on a daily basis. If business as a whole moves up and down regularly, do you think your business will do the same? Of course it will.

So you've got to be prepared to adjust at the drop of a hat. You've got to be able to weather downturns and you've got to realize that upturns will probably be temporary. Then there will be a downturn, but it too will most likely be temporary so long as you adjust in the right ways.

Up-trends or up-turns usually take time to develop. Unfortunately the same cannot be said for downtrends and down-turns. They happen rather abruptly and the descent can be dramatic in a very short period of time.

Again the key is to know this will happen, prepare your self and your business in advance in case of slower growth, and keep on "truck'n".

Secret #4: Hard work is part of the game

I have devoted nearly 40 years of my life to learning and practicing the secrets of home based businesses. I have had my share of failures. I have thought many, many times that a project was mine for the grabbing only to have it yanked out from under me by a faltering economy or a more aggressive competitor or a prospect who just used me for a hidden agenda.

I've had my near misses and my total failures. I've been discouraged. I've been totally confused and bewildered. But I've never given up. Nor should you.

I see people come into the business all the time with unrealistic expectations, thinking that life is just going to hand them a successful business on a silver platter. They've blown in and blown out in short order.

This is a reality check. There is work involved. You've actually got to work at it.

But you've got to make the hard work fun by doing what you love. Life is too short to spend all your best time and effort on something that makes you miserable, even if the money is good.

If there are aspects you don't enjoy doing, or there are aspects you haven't the desire to learn or create, look for people who have already created that product or service for you. Delegate if you must. If you don't want to do the work of creating a website, creating promotional materials or a host of other things, get someone else to do that for you. Concentrate your time on what you enjoy doing, but recognize that you've got to work at it persistently or it has all been for naught.

Secret #5: Model others who are already successful

Don't try to invent everything yourself. Instead look to those successful "10th degree black belt grandmaster home stagers and re-designers" for inspiration. Adapt what they have already created and tweak what already exists to your own needs.

Let the vision and creativity of others propel you into your own unique creative ideas and solutions. None of us get to the top on our own.

Secret #6: Don't put all your eggs in one basket

If you've ever watched a marshal arts type movie or a marshal arts class in progress (I loved the movie "The Last Samurai") then you already know it is commonplace for students and participants to train in a multitude of ways. They prepare for attacks from the front, the sides and from the back. They learn grappling and ground techniques. They learn how to defend themselves against multiple attacks all at the same time. They learn to be ready for all situations.

In business you want to develop multiple streams of income. It is for this reason that I teach 3 types of business ventures: home staging, interior redesign and corporate art consulting. It is for this reason I don't just sell a service, but I've developed a multitude of visual aids and tools.

It's also why I trade in the stock market and the currency market. I practice what I preach: develop multiple streams of income so that if one entity goes down, hopefully the others will go up and sustain you until the correction is over.

Secret #7: Find a mentor or coach for faster results

One of the treasures most appreciated by my students is the on-going support I give, in many cases absolutely free of charge. My philosophy differs from so many competing trainers so I thought you might want to know what that differentiation means to you:

- My discussion forum is free to anyone.

- My business building newsletters are free bonuses to those that purchase my business training directly from me.

- My email support is free.

- There are no recurring monthly or annual fees to my member's only site, to the directory listings, to the monthly decorating tips.

- Mentoring is based on 40+ years of business experience – exceedingly hard to find in this industry where most "trainers" have only been around for a year or two.

The world is full of mentors and coaches. Some are good; others are not. It's up to you to ferret out the good from the weak.

Surviving the First Ten Years

Whether you're operating in a strong economy or a weak one, only 25% of businesses that survive the first year in business will likely still be around in ten years. Not the best of odds is it? Naturally none of us go into business thinking it won't survive over the long haul. But the business climate constantly changes, particularly since the advent of the internet. So here are some tips for helping you make sure your business will still thrive 10 years from now.

You're going to have to ask yourself some tough questions and try to look at your progress as objectively as you can.

1. Have you accomplished your original goals when you first started?
2. If you have not reached your original goals, have you evaluated your business and determined why you have fallen short?
3. Have you determined if your business is growing, stagnant or failing?
4. When was the last time you set or reset your goals?
5. Do you still possess passion for your business and its future?
6. Is your business moving in the right direction?

A top consultant tries to achieve profits by identifying business opportunities and then assembling the necessary finances and resources to turn those opportunities into profits. You do not want to set up your business to  resemble bowling pins ready to be knocked down by the first ball thrown at you. Do you have control over your own destiny? Do you take the initiative with bold creative ideas? Do you have steady cash flow? Do you seek help or advice from professional consultants or advisers?

Let's try to identify your strengths and weaknesses and compare them with your opportunities.

1. Are you providing clients with a unique and rare service or product?
2. Are your services and products needed?
3. Are you making sure your services and products are not obsolete?
4. Are your offerings superior to your competitors?
5. How great is your customer service?
6. What kind of results are you getting from your advertising?
7. Are you concentrated first on serving your target market?
8. Do you seek out other markets as well?
9. Are you professionally informed and trained?
10. Do you have a thorough knowledge of your fixed and variable costs?
11. Do you work to control and reduce expenses?
12. Do you have an excellent profit margin and cash flow?
13. How fast do you collect account receivables?
14. How fast do you pay account payables?
15. Do you limit the number of account payables?
16. Are you prepared for unexpected business needs with extra financial resources?
17. How up to date is your business plan?

Write down the answers to these questions. Fix what needs fixing. Adjust what needs adjusting.

Just as a reminder, let's also list some questions that pertain to why businesses fail.

1. Are your selling prices too high, too low or right on target so that you can generate a net profit?
2. Are your services or products obsolete?
3. Is your cash flow poor or tight?
4. What is the ratio of your expenses to your sales?

5. Is your profit margin non existent?
6. Are you working from home or is your location poor or lacking parking?
7. Is your target market growing or shrinking?
8. What is your geographical location? Rural? Urban?
9. Is your advertising campaign costly or ineffective?
10. Do you have poor credit?
11. Are your managerial and organizational skills poor?
12. Are your interior design skills poor?
13. Are you surrounded by negative people?
14. Is your customer service non-existent or inferior?
15. Is your business name, slogan or brand weak or confusing?
16. Can you recognize whether your business is on the verge of failure?

Take a hard, close look at your business. Fix what needs fixing. Adjust what needs adjustment. If in doubt, get advice.

10 - Getting Paid!
Additional Resources to Promote and Advance Your Business

You don't have to re-invent the wheel when it comes to creating visual aids to augment your portfolio, especially when you are new in your business and don't have the necessary evidence to support your claims. So here is a list of some visual aids, action tools and additional training you might consider to help you further and eliminate the frustrations and time needed to create your own.

Additional Training of Value

Home Staging for Profit
Basic Home Staging training manual. Get the best selling book on how to start a home staging business and build a six figure income. Secrets of home stagers on how to start, develop, grow, manage and sustain a home staging business.

Available as ebook or as printed manual (256 pgs). Updated yearly.

Staging Luxurious Homes
Secrets of developing a clientele among the affluent homeowners in any geographical area. Teaches different psychological idiosyncrasies and

requirements of wealthy prospects and clients and how to build a lucrative business in this market (232 pgs).

Staging Portfolio Secrets

This guide teaches you not only how to create a powerful, effective portfolio to use to garner new clients and show off your talents, but it teaches you a fun, non-threatening method of getting face-to-face appointments with the very people who have the need and ability to hire you to manage their projects and also have the power and authority to refer you on to other people who also have the ability to hire you. (260 pgs)

Home Staging for Yourself

Thorough checklist of the most common home staging tasks suitable for most home situations. The perfect consultation guide which eliminates the need for preparing follow-up reports (80 pgs). Can be sold as part of a consultation service or as a stand-alone product with great perceived value. Pass-through costs so these guides are free to stagers. Stagers can purchase them in small quantities of 5-10 at a time and up-charge for them to make a profit. You should always have an ample supply of these handy checklist guides with you at all times.

Rearrange It!

Basic Interior Redesign training. Secrets of re-designers on how to start, develop, grow, manage and sustain an interior redesign or one day decorating business. Available as ebook or in printed manual (176 pgs).

Décor Secrets Revealed

Twenty five chapters on the secrets, concepts and strategies used by professional stagers and re-designers to arrange furniture and accessories. Concepts are traditionally accepted practices of interior designers everywhere (25 chapters). Over 500 color images. Available solely as an ebook and must be read on your computer. This ebook is not compatible with Mac computers.

Arrange Your Stuff

The sequel to Décor Secrets Revealed, this workbook expands and emphasizes the concepts already presented. Shows multiple ways to use the same furnishings in the same room to achieve several different arrangement ideas. Great for keeping handy when on appointments to stimulate ideas (188 pgs).

Where There's a Wall – There's a Way (new version coming)

101 ways to dress a naked wall – this handy guide shows anyone how to arrange beautiful wall groupings. First published in 1986, it has been revamped and updated (cover design might be different from what's pictured here). Covers the general design concepts of arranging simple to highly complex wall groupings. Especially useful training for interior re-designers. Fully illustrated with line drawings and plenty of photos (128 pgs approx).

Advanced Redesign

Once your business is off the ground and you've gotten your feet wet, you might want to discover additional great techniques and tactics for getting the most profits from your business you can. This manual (or ebook) teaches you how to take your business to the next level for even more profit (200 pgs).

Upgrade to One of Our Courses

 Many students get introduced to our products and training by running across a stand-alone or "a la carte" product, not knowing that we offer comprehensive certification courses. We have several to choose from based on your goals, your background and experience level. Please visit our website for detailed information. If you'd like to upgrade to a course that includes duplicates, let us know before you make your selection and we'll be happy to substitute another product so you don't get a duplication of products. You'll have to call us at (714) 963-3071 so we can place your order manually or make a notation in the Notes box during the checkout process and ask for a substitution so you don't get duplicate products to what you've already purchased. We will contact you and let you know your options before sending out your course products.

For current list of products and services available, please visit our handy checklist page at: http://www.decorate-redecorate.com/home-staging-redesign.html.

Additional Visual Aids and Tools

Musical Slide Show CDs on Home Staging

Showing before and after pictures of staged homes of every income bracket, along with the probable benefits usually received by home staging services, this slideshow helps prospects see the differences staging has made for other owners. Has musical background. Great for loaning to someone to show to their spouse.

Powerpoint Presentation CD on Home Staging

Series of before and after pictures of staged homes from varying income brackets in a Powerpoint Presentation. Developed to show to real estate agents to show the win/win approach of utilizing staging services to sell their clients home. Comes with a fully developed and editable script and slides.

Musical Slide Show CDs on Interior Redesign

Series of before and after pictures of actual homes that have benefited from an interior redesign service. Homes are of varying income brackets across the USA. Musical background. Great for loaning to a prospect to show their spouse.

Powerpoint Presentation on Interior Redesign

Series of before and after pictures in a Powerpoint Presentation on CD. Useful in making presentations to a group. Comes will fully developed editable script.

Postcards on Services

Variety of professionally designed and printed postcards to assist in announcing your business, pointing out the benefits of your services and the need for such services. Generic. Sold in sets of 100 per design. Several styles and messages to choose from.

Postcards Announcing Certification Achievement

Professionally designed and printed postcards to announce the achievement of a CSS and/or CRS designation. CSS is our Certified Staging Specialist designation; CRS is our Certified Redesign Specialist designation. These cards available only to officially certified stagers and re-designers in our program once certification requirements have been met.

Presentation Folders and Matching Letterhead

Handsome folders with matching letterhead and matching referral cards. Designed and professionally printed for home stagers and interior re-designers. Currently two styles to choose from.

Many Additional Resources

We are constantly developing new resources ourselves and constantly on the lookout for resources available by other companies. Our shopping cart always has the up-to-the-minute products and pricing. You can access our catalog and cart by visiting: http://www.decorate-redecorate.com/catalog.html

Contact Information

For further information or to acquire any of my products or courses and books to help you advance your business, please visit: **www.decorate-redecorate.com**

I hope you have learned not only how to protect yourself in all your business dealings, but how to use your strategies and positioning to impress your clients and ward off difficulties others might encounter – especially your competitors. Any time you can better prepare yourself, better protect yourself, better administer your procedures, you're well ahead of your average competitor.

Most people start a business with little to no experience and often do so with unrealistic goals, failure to follow through, and failure to abide by solid business procedures. Many of the people you compete with today will not be around in the industry 10 years from now. I hope you will. I think I've given you some tools that will make that much more likely.

Your kind words of encouragement and referrals are always welcome with gratitude. I'm never too busy to take care of the needs of any person you refer.

Best wishes for a rewarding and protected journey.

Barbara Jennings, CSS/CRS
Author/Mentor

Printed in the United States
134507LV00003B/9/P